T0291415

Beyond Rationality in Organization and Management

Spanning the 20th and 21st centuries, the writers considered in this first book of the *Routledge Focus on Women Writers in Organization Studies* series make an important contribution to how we think about rationality in managing, leading and working. It provides a space in which to think differently about rationality, challenging dominant masculine logics while positioning relations between people centre stage.

A critical and intellectually provocative text, the book provides a nuanced and practical account of rationality in organizational contexts, making it clear that women have and continue to write groundbreaking work on the subject: women like Lillian Moller Gilbreth, who was at the forefront of developments in scientific management, and Frances Perkins, who was the first female US cabinet secretary. Both are important not only for what they achieved but also as illustrations of the ways in which women have been written out of the accounts of managing and management thought. This matters not only because credit is denied to those who deserve it, but also because it impoverishes our understanding of complex organizational phenomenon. Where so much extant writing on managing and organizing is preoccupied with abstract notions of structure, strategy, metaphor and machines, the writers considered here explain why effective working and managing is primarily about seeing and working with people. Writers such as Arlie Hochschild, Mary Parker Follett and Heather Höpfl remind us that rationality cannot be decoupled from emotion or, where a system is to be rationalised, then it should start with and enhance the lives of people – be designed with people at the centre. In this sense, the book is not arguing for a wholesale rejection of rationality. Rather, authors call on readers to move beyond a preoccupation with rationality for its own sake, seeing it instead as a useful and highly contestable aspect of organizational life.

Each woman writer is introduced and analysed by an expert in their field. Further reading and accessible resources are also identified for those interested in knowing more. This book will be relevant to students, researchers and practitioners with an interest in business and management, organizational studies, critical management studies, gender studies and sociology. Like all the books in this series, it will also be of interest to anyone who wants to see, think and act differently.

Robert McMurray is Professor of Work and Organization at The York Management School, UK. Research interests include the organization of health care, professions, emotion labour, dirty work and visual methods. Other collaborative book projects include *The Dark Side of Emotional Labour* (2015), *The Management of Wicked Problems in Health and Social Care* (2018) and *Urban Portraits* (2017).

Alison Pullen is Professor of Management and Organization Studies at Macquarie University, Australia, and Editor in Chief of *Gender, Work and Organization*. Alison's research has been concerned with analysing and intervening in the politics of work as it concerns gender discrimination, identity politics and organizational injustice.

Routledge Focus on Women Writers in Organization Studies
Edited by Robert McMurray and Alison Pullen

Given that women and men have always engaged in and thought about organizing, why is it that core management texts are dominated by the writing of men? This series redresses the neglect of women in organization thought and practice and highlights their contributions. Through a selection of carefully curated short-form books, it covers major themes such as structure, rationality, managing, leading, culture, power, ethics, diversity and sustainability; and also attends to contemporary debates surrounding performativity, the body, emotion, materiality and post-coloniality. Individually, each book provides stand-alone coverage of a key sub-area within organization studies, with a contextual series introduction written by the editors. Collectively, the titles in the series give a global overview of how women have shaped organizational thought.

Routledge Focus on Women Writers in Organization Studies will be relevant to students and researchers across business and management, organizational studies, critical management studies, gender studies and sociology.

Beyond Rationality in Organization and Management
Edited by Robert McMurray and Alison Pullen

Power, Politics and Exclusion in Organization and Management
Edited by Robert McMurray and Alison Pullen

For more information about this series, please visit: www.routledge.com/Routledge-Focus-on-Women-Writers-in-Organization-Studies/book-series/RFWWOS

Beyond Rationality in Organization and Management

Edited by Robert McMurray and Alison Pullen

Routledge
Taylor & Francis Group

LONDON AND NEW YORK

First published 2019
by Routledge
2 Park Square, Milton Park, Abingdon, Oxon OX14 4RN

and by Routledge
52 Vanderbilt Avenue, New York, NY 10017

Routledge is an imprint of the Taylor & Francis Group, an informa business

British Library Cataloguing-in-Publication Data
A catalogue record for this book is available from the British Library

Library of Congress Cataloging-in-Publication Data
Names: McMurray, Robert, 1972– editor. | Linstead, Alison, 1971– editor.
Title: Beyond rationality in organization and management / edited by
    Robert McMurray & Alison Pullen.
Description: Abingdon, Oxon ; New York, NY : Routledge, 2019. |
    Series: Routledge focus on women writers on organization studies |
    Includes bibliographical references and index.
Identifiers: LCCN 2019012222 (print) | LCCN 2019013964 (ebook) |
    ISBN 9780429279652 (eBook) | ISBN 9780367233938 (hardback :
    alk. paper)
Subjects: LCSH: Management—Study and teaching. | Organizational
    sociology—Study and teaching. | Women social scientists.
Classification: LCC HD30.4 (ebook) | LCC HD30.4 .B49 2019 (print) |
    DDC 302.3/5—dc23
LC record available at https://lccn.loc.gov/2019012222

ISBN: 978-0-367-23393-8 (hbk)
ISBN: 978-0-429-27965-2 (ebk)

Typeset in Times New Roman
by Apex CoVantage, LLC

Contents

Series note

This series arose from the question: given that women and men have always engaged in and thought about organizing, why are core management texts dominated by the writing of men? Relatedly, and centrally to the development of organization studies as a field, the following questions become key: Why do so few women theorists and writers appear in our lectures and classes on managing, organizing and working? Why have the contribution of women to organization theory been neglected – indeed, written out of – the everyday conversations of the academy?

This series redresses the neglect of women in organization thought and practice. It does so by highlighting the unique contributions of women in respect to fundamental organizational issues such as structure, rationality, managing, leading, culture, power, ethics, diversity and sustainability, while also attending to more nuanced organizational concerns arising from issues such as performativity, the body, emotion, materiality and post-coloniality.

Through a selection of carefully curated short-form books, the series provides an overview of how women have shaped organizational thought. This series is international in scope, drawing on ideas, concepts, experiences and writing from across Europe, North America and Australasia and spanning more than 150 years. As the series develops, our ambition is to move beyond even these confines to encompass the work of women from all parts of the globe.

This is not a standard textbook. It does not offer a chronological history of women in organization theory. It does not (indeed, cannot) claim to be the complete or the last word on women in organization: the contribution of women to organization theory and practice continues and grows. We do not even promise that each chapter will be written like the one that preceded it! Why? It is because the variation in style and substance of each chapter deliberately reflects the varied, exciting and often transgressive women discussed. Indeed, one of the points of this series is to draw attention to the possibility that there are as many ways of thinking about, writing on and doing organizing as there are people. If you want to read and think differently about management work and organization, then this is the series for you.

Readers of this and other volumes in the series will note that the first person is often employed in our accounts of women writers. Reference is made to meetings with writers, to the personal impact of their thinking, and the ways in which writers have moved or challenged their researchers personally. Once again, this personal emotional approach to assessing the work of others is at with odds with more positivistic or masculine approaches that contend that the researcher or analyst of organizations is to remain outside, beyond or above the subject matter – an expert eye whose authorial tone allows them to act as dispassionate judge on the work of others. We argue that the fallacy of neutrality that results from such masculine positivism hides the arbitrary and inherently biased nature of subject selection, appraisal and writing. Just as importantly, it tends to produce sterile prose that does little to convey the excitement and dynamism of the ideas being discussed.

The subject matter of this book has been chosen because the chapter creators believe them to be important, and particular thought has been given to the selection of the women writers shared with you. Authors recognise the bias inherent in any writing project; it is writ large in the series title (*Focus on Women Writers*) and is more explicit in some chapters than others. In editing this series we have been struck with the enthusiasm that informs how our authors have chosen influential women writers, and this enthusiasm can be read in the ways in which the chapters engage with the work of specific writers, the application of these writers to organization studies and the personal reflections of the influence of writers on their own research. The perspective from which we – and our authors – write is therefore open for you (the reader) to read, acknowledge and account for in the multiple ways intended. The lack of consistency with which the authors address fundamental organizational issues should not be read as lacking rigour, but should rather bring an alternative way of leveraging critical thinking through an engaged, personal approach to the field. In this way, authors embody the ideas and ethos of the women writers chosen. While written in an accessible form, each chapter is based on years of engagement with the works of particular writers and an in-depth appreciation of their contribution to and impact on organization studies. There is also critique. The omissions or controversies that have accompanied the work of particular writers is addressed, along with challenges to their work.

The result is a collection of books on women writers that is scholarly, readable and engaging. They introduce you to some of the most important concepts in organization studies from some of the best theorists in the field. Politically and ethically, we hope that this book will help students, lecturers and practitioners reverse a trend that has seen women writers written out of organization theory. Just as importantly, the inclusion of such work usefully challenges many long-held beliefs within mainstream management literature. We hope that this series will be the beginning of your own personal journey of ideas – the text and suggesting readings produced in this book offering a starting point for your own discoveries.

The *Routledge Focus on Women Writers in Organization Studies* series will be relevant to students, teachers and researchers across business and management, organizational studies, critical management studies, gender studies and sociology.

Robert McMurray and Alison Pullen

Contributors

Valerie Caven is Senior Lecturer at Nottingham Business School, Nottingham Trent University, UK. Research interests include gender and employment, particularly women in male-dominated spheres of work, and the transfer of equality/diversity policy into practice. Recently she has co-edited and contributed to three volumes on *Hidden Inequalities in the Workplace* as part of the *Stigma in the Workplace Series*.

Nottingham Business School, Nottingham
Trent University, UK
valerie.caven@ntu.ac.uk

Achilleas Karayiannis has recently joined the Aston Business School, UK, as Teaching Fellow in the Department of Work & Organisational Psychology. His doctoral research thesis focused on the application of Brecht's Epic Theatre and Stanislavski's method in a service-oriented context. His research interests also extend to the use of the theatre metaphor in an organizational context.

Department of Work & Organisational Psychology,
Aston Business School, UK
a.karayiannis@aston.ac.uk

Monika Kostera is Professor Ordinaria and Chair of Management at the Jagiellonian University in Kraków, Poland, and Linnaeus University, Sweden. She has been Professor and Chair at Durham University, UK. She holds two titular professorships in economics and the humanities. Her research interests include organizational imagination, disalienated work and ethnography. She has also published three poetry collections.

Jagiellonian University, Kraków, Poland
monika.kostera@uj.edu.pl

Scott Lawley is Senior Lecturer in Organisation Studies at Nottingham Trent University, UK. His research interests include equality and diversity practice, especially regarding LGBT+ participation in the sports industry. He is the co-author, with Professor Daniel King, of the textbook *Organizational Behaviour*.

Nottingham Business School, Nottingham Trent University, UK
scott.lawley@ntu.ac.uk

Robert McMurray is Professor of Work and Organisation at The York Management School, UK. Research interests include the organization of health care, professions, emotion labour, dirty work and visual methods. Other collaborative book projects include *The Dark Side of Emotional Labour* (Routledge), *The Management of Wicked Problems in Health and Social Care* (Routledge) and *Urban Portraits*.

The York Management School, University of York, UK
robert.mcmurray@york.ac.uk

Albert J. Mills, PhD, is Professor of Management and the former director of the PhD (Management) Program at Saint Mary's University, Canada. He is the author of 45 books and edited collections and is currently the co-editor of *Qualitative Research in Organizations and Management* and co-chair of the International Critical Studies Association.

Sobey School of Business, Saint Mary's University, Canada
albert.mills@smu.ca

Ellen O'Connor is Senior Research Fellow at the Institute for Leadership Studies, Barowsky School of Business, Dominican University of California, USA. She explores creative relating between the humanities and management. She has experimented with literary, historical and philosophical frameworks and methods. In particular, she has focused on the contemporary as well as historical significance of classic texts and authors.

Barowsky School of Business, Dominican University of California,
USA
ellen.oconnnor@dominican.edu

Alison Pullen is Professor of Management and Organization Studies at Macquarie University, Australia, and Editor in Chief of *Gender, Work and Organization*. Alison's research has been concerned with analysing and intervening in the politics of work as it concerns gender discrimination, identity politics and organizational injustice.

Department of Management, Macquarie University, Australia
alison.pullen@mq.edu.au

Jenna Ward is Associate Professor of Work, Organization and Emotion at the University of Leicester, UK, School of Business. Her research focuses on exploring emotionality within organizations. Prioritising marginalised voices, Jenna employs and develops innovative arts-based research methods that complement her ethnographically informed research designs to observe and probe beyond the surface of individual experiences of work, organizing and organizations. Areas of interest include emotional labour, dirty work, emotional dirty work, visual and arts-based methods, creative industries, health care, death work and the management and organization of voluntary work and volunteers.

School of Business, University of Leicester, Leicester, UK
jw704@le.ac.uk

Kristin S. Williams is a PhD candidate in management at the Sobey School of Business at Saint Mary's University,Canada, and the CEO and president of Junior Achievement of Nova Scotia. She is the past chair of the Community Sector Council of Nova Scotia and sits on the advisory board for Nova Scotia's Centre for Employment Innovation.

Sobey School of Business, Saint Mary's University, Canada
kristin@pathcommunications.ca

1 Introduction

Beyond rationality in organization and management

Robert McMurray and Alison Pullen

Management has long been concerned with the appearance and practice of rationality in organizations. Much academic research and practitioner writing has focused on developing prescriptions for the most efficient means to a given end, while searches for and claims to rational management are writ large accounts of bureaucratic ideal types, scientific management, just-in-time production, total quality management, decision-making, recruitment and selection of human resources, and business process reengineering (to name but a few systems and practices). While this concern is most readily associated with the "founding fathers" of management theory such as Weber, Taylor, Fayol and latterly Ritzer, foundational women such as Mary Parker Follett, Lillian Moller Gilbreth and Frances Perkins made early contributions to our understanding of the nature and effects of rational organizing. Accounts of the history of management tend to underplay the contribution of women to the development of the field and to organization theory and practice. The marginalisation of contemporary women writers such as Arlie Russell Hochschild and Heather Höpfl – whose work problematises uncritical acceptance of rationality as neutral, desirable or separable from emotion, people and the wider world – continues.

The result of such exclusion and marginalisation is that the work of women writers on the subject of rationality is often poorly understood, under-taught or forgotten, such that the subtlety and insight of their thinking has been overlooked, lost or oversimplified. This book addresses this deficit, as chapter authors detail how such women writers have reshaped our understanding through detailed analysis, critique and repositioning of rationality. This collection reminds us that rationality is just one perspective on, or feature of, organizing. Moreover, it is a perspective which is partial in the absence of a concern with emotion, culture, aesthetics, ethics, agency and collaboration.

Spanning the 20th and 21st centuries, the writers considered in this *Routledge Focus on Women Writers in Organization Studies Series* make an important contribution to how we manage, lead and work today. Specifically, the book provides a more nuanced and practical account of rationality in organizational contexts. Together the chapters make clear that women have and continue to write groundbreaking work on the subject, providing concepts for thinking differently about rationality and its place in managing and leading. A central commitment of such work is giving voice to those who would seek to challenge dominant masculine logics of rationality.

What the chapters in this book have in common is a reminder that organizations are first and foremost about people. Where so much extant writing on managing and organizing is preoccupied with abstract notions of structure, strategy, metaphor and machines, the writers considered here explain why effective working and managing is primarily about seeing and working with people. They highlight the ways in which creativity, conflict and endeavour emerge from the spaces between people, and that effective organizing and managing is about relating to people. At times this means resisting the suffocating strictures of rationalising tendencies that position people as little more than cogs within the machine. At other times it requires an acknowledgement that rationality cannot be decoupled from emotion or, where a system is to be rationalised, then it should start with and enhance the lives of people – be designed with people at the centre. In this sense, the book is not arguing for a wholesale rejection of rationality. Rather, authors call on its readers to move beyond a preoccupation with rationality for its own sake, seeing it instead as one useful and highly contestable aspect of organizational life. Authors also challenge us to recognise that certain rationalising tendencies have the effect of writing out the theories, work and contributions of particular individuals on the basis on their gender, colour, religion or geography. Such tendencies diminish our understanding of the range, complexity and beauty of organizational life. This book is an attempt to respect women writers, showing the diverse contributions they have made to the ways we think about organizations today.

Exemplifying this, Chapter 2 offers new insight into one of the best-known and foundational women thinkers on managing and organizing: Mary Parker Follett. Ellen O'Connor's close reading of Mary Parker Follett's work directs our attention to the concept of dynamic relating and the important place it held in Follett's thinking. Dynamic relating is described as a concern with the power of "purposive action and will" that drives toward unifying rather than fragmentary experiences (be this in respect to the actions of individuals or groups). We come to understand the ways in which Mary Parker Follett is concerned with creativity, continual becoming and relational effects that unfold as people, process and environments interact to create the world anew. There is a sense of holism in Follett's work that leads her to criticise rational attempts to freeze and separate out the components of dynamic relations in order to unpick and understand their nature. Such atomising necessarily overlooks and "tears to pieces" processual webs of creativity: it ignores the spaces between people – the spaces where creativity takes place and collectively becomes meaningful. As O'Connor notes, Follett's work goes beyond the realms of management (as a role description) to encompass the study of relations and unbounded potential in the functioning of society as a whole. Mary Parker Follett encourages us to see our interdependencies and interrelations as they pertain to democracy, leading, managing, learning, the division of labour and so much more. In her attempt to break down the artificial boundaries between people and statuses, Follett tackles issues that some areas of mainstream management are only now starting to grasp some three-quarters of a century later.

Interdependencies and interrelations are also considered in Chapter 3 as Jenna Ward explores the fundamental contributions of sociologist Arlie Russell Hochschild to organization theory, focusing on her central role in advancing understanding of the relation between private lives and public organizing. Arlie Hochschild is described as having founded the sociology of emotion. Perhaps best known for the development of emotional labour as a concept, Arlie Hochschild effectively dismantles the notion that emotion is antithetical to organizing. Arlie Hochschild's research demonstrates the ways in which feelings and emotional displays are routinely manipulated in return for a wage as part of a "rational commodification of emotions". The chapter considers whether the commodification involved in emotional labour is always and necessarily harmful to the worker, pointing out that very different approaches to the issue are taken depending on whether researchers adopt a sociological or psychological framing. As the chapter draws to a close, Ward reminds us that Arlie Hochschild's writing goes well beyond emotion to encompass assessments of the balance between work and wider life (effectively pointing, once again, to the arbitrary nature of the boundaries drawn between rationality and emotion, work and home). Arlie Hochschild's significant writings are thus presented as essential reading for anyone seeking to understand what it means to live and work under global capitalism, whether considered in macro, meso or micro terms.

In Chapter 4, Scott Lawley and Valerie Caven review the work and life of Lillian Moller Gilbreth. While Lillian Moller Gilbreth is appreciated for her work on scientific management and motion studies, her wider contribution to the study and practice of organization and management is less well understood. This chapter considers how her thinking has tended to be marginalised and overshadowed by the privileging of male voices, such that her husband Frank is more readily acknowledged for their joint work on motion studies, while Fredrick Taylor and Elton Mayo dominate accounts of scientific management and human relations – both areas in which it could be argued that Lillian Gilbreth led the way. That Lillian is less well known for such work is attributed by Lawley and Caven to a double erasure, through which Lillian's gender is neutralised and her field-leading influence left unrecognised or trivialised. We learn that despite university systems that were prejudicial to obtaining her doctorate, and having primary responsibility for the care of a large family, Lillian Moller Gilbreth informed the management of engineering, health care, retail and the home while promoting understanding of issues that would become classic organizational concerns. This included highlighting the importance of group norms, emotional fatigue, ergonomics, work-life balance, employment law and consumer behaviour. This extended to one of the earliest large-scale pieces of market research on menstruation that went on to inform concerns with the embodied nature of work. The chapter concludes by noting that Lillian Moller Gilbreth was a true polymath whose continued relevance to organization studies is well worth revisiting, not least because she advocated designing rational systems that worked for and benefited people (rather than the other way around).

As we move to Chapter 5, Achilleas Karayiannis and Monika Kostera consider how the work of Heather Höpfl disrupts standard (rational) accounts of organization and management. The very structure and writing of this chapter reflects and embodies the disruptive sensibility of Heather Höpfl. Rather than offering us academic context, neat abstract or lists of authoritative quotes, Karayiannis and Kostera open with a poem by Heather Höpfl on the tyranny of taxonomy, ordering, lists and organizing. From the beginning, the point is made that organizing is social, political and personal – that in order to understand the world around us, we need to relate to the people who constitute our worlds. To this end, we are offered two very personal accounts of the impact of Heather Höpfl's approach to relating to others. The result is to put people centre stage in our accounts of organizing, whether this be in respect of feelings, beliefs, learning, culture, politics or resistance. A significant portion of the chapter is devoted to Heather Höpfl's writing on theatre and organization, with particular attention to the ways in which a dramaturgical lens can inform our understanding of managing, working, performing and sense-making. This brings to the fore the importance of "emptiness" – a concept and space rarely considered in mainstream account managing whose rhetorics often strive to simplify our complex worlds with accounts of linearity, rational procedure and imposed structure. This, then, is a chapter that challenges us to think again about what it means to organize – to go beyond the rhetoric of rationality and to follow Heather Höpfl's example; namely, to experience, write about and enact organizing as drama, poetry, metaphor and relation.

We conclude this collection with Kristin S. Williams and Albert J. Mills, who seek to rediscover the voice of Frances Perkins, the first female US cabinet secretary). In so doing, they disrupt the silence and storytelling that have so far written Frances Perkins out of, or fundamentally adjusted her position in, history, managing and organizing. In reconstructing accounts of Frances Perkins's actions and relations, the chapter ably demonstrates the role of history in gendering organizational acts and actors, particularly where the main protagonists are women. We come to understand how language, subjectivity and power are employed in the positioning (marginalisation) of individuals who are different, such that their innovations and achievements are attributed to others. Williams and Mills demonstrate the ways in which different narrations of Perkins's life say as much about the agendas of commentators who would use Frances to promote narratives of heroism, feminism, conflict, controversy or acquiescence. In so doing, they remind us that one is not judged simply by one's words, acts and deeds but also through the interpretations and narrations of those with the power to revoice a life. This is an issue of power, for as the authors note, when "women take up malestream roles, there persists a drive to subjugate them back into subject positions which are consistent with taken-for-granted gender attributes and behaviour". This chapter – and the wider series – is as response to that drive.

The chapter on Frances Perkins neatly brings us back to one of the central themes of this *Routledge Focus on Women Writers in Organization Studies Series*, namely, the need to reclaim the work and contributions of those women who have been lost to or written out of management studies. Through their work we will never think of rationality, managing or organizing the same way again.

2 Unbounded relationality

Mary Parker Follett's integrative theory, method and life

Ellen O'Connor

> We are not now master of our experience; we do not know what it is and we could not express it if we did. We need an articulate experience . . . from such experiments a new type of leadership might appear.
>
> (Follett, 1924: 216)

Mary Parker Follett (1868–1933) was a management theorist, organizational leader, political scientist, community organizer and social entrepreneur, among other titles. But in light of Joan Tonn's definitive biography (Tonn, 2003), Follett is best understood as pursuing a way of life that she called creative experience (Follett, 1924). Creative experience is the generating and freeing of energy through dynamic relating, whereby interdependent elements work to achieve greater unity within and among themselves. For example, as an organizational member unifies with the team and the organization, all entities become more whole, independently and interdependently. Follett called this wholemaking.

In this chapter, I use this principle to understand Follett's life, theory and method. Looking at each of these threads individually and interdependently gives the best understanding. Cabot (1934) stated that in all her scholarly and executive work, Follett sought to understand dynamic relating. However, he did not emphasise Follett's method of collapsing the boundaries between scientific practice, including both theory building and experimentation, and daily living. I go further to argue that she would understand dynamic relating not only scientifically and professionally but also intimately, as her way of life. After a brief introduction to Follett's concepts and approach, I discuss her biography as an exemplar of dynamic relating.

Key concepts

Dynamic relating engages "the power of thinking, purposing, willing" (1924: 57) "those fundamental values for which most of us . . . are really living" (Metcalf & Urwick, 1940: 268). Experience thus becomes "the dynamo station" (1924: 85). The process scales from smaller to larger units and from immediate to remote situations. The opposite of dynamic relating is lost energy due to fragmentation. Follett focused on transitions where lives hung in the balance between uniting and separating: immigrants becoming citizens, adolescents becoming adults, entry-level workers advancing – or not. In a human relations sense, she pursued the creative possibilities of membership. More broadly and theoretically, she pursued the creative prospects inherent in any situation that is seen as a whole made up of interdependent parts.

It is impossible to know Follett's personal experience of creative experience. But there is enough evidence to build a case. I maintain that Follett experienced divisive tensions in herself and in her relating of herself to her environment such that she felt compelled to find a creative solution. These tensions include (1) the gap between the society she lived in and the one she wanted to live in, a society that she could readily envision and begin creating; (2) the continuing costs of the gap to herself, others and her society; (3) the persistent failure of established institutions to recognise and close the gap; (4) the emergence of energies, coalescing into social movements and experiments, with potential to close the gap; and (5) her growing appreciation of her success with (4) and an increasingly strategic vision of her contribution.

Of course, Follett pursued her understanding of creative experience along conventional lines. She studied the evidence in several disciplines, notably psychology and physiology, and in the theoretical, experimental and applied sciences. She found further support in contemporary political and cultural as well as scientific developments. Physiologists had found that muscular activity partially produced the stimulus that was said to cause muscular activity. They posited the reflex arc, the "path of the stimulations received in consequence of a function of the individual itself" (1924: 59). Follett built on Edwin Holt's extension of this principle to Freudian psychology. Holt held that suppression is a division within the self. The individual does not act with his whole heart, and "a part of his strength has always to be spent in suppressing dissociated and antagonistic tendencies" (Holt, 1915: 122). Holt associated suppression with the "anomalies, contradictions, perplexities" that accompany any new experience. He proposed free play of opposing tendencies, so that "they meet each other, and a line of conduct emerges which is dictated by both sets of motives together, and which embodies all that [is] not downright antagonistic in the two" (Holt, 1915: 122).

For Follett, a key finding was that the reflex arc is the path of stimuli received *as a result of the individual's own activity*, "thus experience is given us as self-creating coherence" (1924: 61). She took this insight to scale, studying how individuals cooperate to make neighbourhoods, cities, and other collectivities that make individuals who cooperate to make collectivities that cooperate and so forth.

My response is to an environment which is changing because of the activity between it and me; and that function may be continuously modified by itself; my activity itself may change my activity. By this interlocking activity, individual and situation each is creating itself anew, and thus relating themselves anew, giving us the evolving situation.

(1924: 89)

The circular reflex operates on "infra-personal, personal and social levels". Social psychology must study how this law applies to social processes. "[T]he activity of the individual is only in a certain sense caused by the stimulus of the situation because that activity is itself helping to produce the situation which causes the activity of the individual". We cannot catch the stimulus stimulating or the response responding. Cause and effect are ways of describing moments in an ongoing situation when we separate those moments from the larger whole (1924: 59–61). This separation does not shed light on the larger situation or process. In fact, we "tear [experience] to pieces" by designating subject and object, stimulus and response, instead of recognising "interplay of forces" (1924: 74–75).

Follett saw no benefit to isolating phenomena. That would only block her understanding of reality or, better put, her understanding of what matters in understanding reality. Instead of inquiring about a good society and how to make it, she asked how "society" and "society-making" could be meaningful to herself and others. The word "society" is made meaningful by seeing "society" as a creative possibility for oneself:

[W]e see in a given instance that we can easily make our influence potent if we would do certain things, but are we willing to do these things? It depends on whether we care most for my way or your way, or for the whole psychic significance of that which is connected by myriad threads with every other situation in life.

(1924: 190)

The principle applies to the most basic beliefs and to common sense.

There is no use chasing through the universe for a "real" you or a "real" me; it is more useful to study our interactions, these are certainly real. What happens when I meet another person for the first time? He comes to me always pushing in front of him his picture of himself; as I get to know him, do I see that picture gradually disappear, leaving his real self? Not at all, I put my own interpretative picture in its place. Where, then, is the real person – for me? It is in his behaving (and his account of his behaving is part of his behavior) plus my interpretation of his behavior *as shown by my behaving.*

(1924: 177, emphasis in original)

Through circular response, "we are creating each other all the time" (1924: 62–63).

Follett could have been talking about herself when she described the role of the political architect:

> The political scientist may record the level of the moment which the interweaving of response and situation is attaining. The political philosopher may presage the tendencies of the strivings and their possible fulfillment. But the political architect, the statesman who takes these living concepts into the arena of factual happenings and makes them part of the interplay of concrete reciprocal servings, shows us the full creative process of his world. It is he who welds the generating centres of the community into cooperating creatings of new factual happenings and new awareness – the ceaseless progress of existence.

(1924: 231)

This sentence is a mouthful, but it shows how Follett made her experience creative. The key is boundarylessness. To explain this, I juxtapose her with Herbert Simon.

Simon separated management from economics. In particular, he reworked economics' rational man into management's boundedly rational man. He also imposed the construct of organization as a constraint in order to work out this man. "Boundedly rational actors had . . . to limit the context of action before it could be analyzed" (Spender, 2013: 336). Simon's method thus required that the scientist be just as boundedly rational as the object of study. His focus, then, was boundedly rational man as opposed to rational man, enabled by the construct of organization, and the new field of management and organization science as opposed to classical economics.

Follett went further, to collapse the boundaries that Simon would impose in conceptualising the individual and defining the field. First, as explained earlier, she drew no boundary between scientific practice and creative experience (way of life). Second, for Follett, boundary-setting is not useful as an end in itself and does not accomplish any finality. If it advances whole-making it is helpful, but only in light of the larger endeavour. Third, her interest in business was not because she sought to understand management or organization, but because she saw it as a laboratory for understanding human relations generally and collective creativeness specifically (Metcalf & Urwick, 1940: 93–94).

Relating to Follett

Binding and bonding have limited and limiting uses. We need counteracting methods for "watching varying activities in their relatings to other varying activities" (1924: 68). This observation applies to understanding Follett herself. Thus I must address a barrier to meeting Follett. Today, she seems excessively idealistic and there is a tendency to condescend toward her.

She has been called a utopian (Nohria, 1995: 162) and a romantic (Kanter, 1995: xviii). Follett received this criticism in her lifetime:

> I hope you do not think that I am taking a rose-coloured view of business. Indeed, I am not. I am perfectly aware that in most plants the attitude is, "I'm the boss. You do what I say". But, aware as I am of that, at the same time I see signs of something else, and it is on these signs that I am placing my hopes.
>
> (Metcalf & Urwick, 1940: 269)

Nohria and Kanter wrote before Tonn (2003), which proved Follett's solid grounding in reality. Yet the fact remains that Follett upheld ideas and ideals that are not widely celebrated today, and she did so enthusiastically.

She avowed her belief in laws of human conduct that follow from nature. "The fundamental law of the universe is the increase of life, the development of human powers, and either you keep yourself in obedience to that law or for you the universe breaks around you and is shattered" (Metcalf & Urwick, 1940: 182). "The biological law is growth by the continuous integration of simple, specific responses; in the same way do we build up our characters by uniting diverse tendencies into new action patterns; social progress follows exactly the same law" (1924: 174). The "alpha and omega of philosophical teaching [is that] nature desires eagerly opposites and out of them completes its harmony" (Follett, 1918: 34). "The core of the development, expansion, growth, progress of humanity is the confronting and gripping of opposites" (1924: 302). Self-government is the law of our being (1924: 204). Every living process is subject to its own authority, that is, the authority evolved by, or involved in, the process of relating (1924: 206). Every individual must learn the relation of self-activity to the attainment of desires and creation of "finer and finer wants" and "the possibilities of fresh satisfactions" (1924: 80–81, 204, 230).

She proclaimed her belief in progress, that the hardest problems could be solved. She would work on "the greatest task man has been given", to "solve the problems of human relations" (Metcalf & Urwick, 1940: 269). She saw herself living in a time of great promise and rejoiced in the possibilities. She hailed a "moment in creating when evolution turns a corner":

> [W]e are now at the beginning of a period of creative energy . . . instead of being the individual creativeness of the past which gave us our artists and our poets, we may now enter on a period of collective creativeness if we have the imagination to see its potentialities, its reach, its ultimate significance, above all if we are willing patiently to work out the method.
>
> (Metcalf & Urwick, 1940: 94)

She held that the federalist principle of democracy is conducive to creative experience (1924: 101, 111). She applauded "correspondences in thinking between scientists, philosophers, and business managers", which show "we are on the right track". When "people studying relations from such totally different angles come to the same conclusions, it seems to me of the greatest significance" (Metcalf & Urwick, 1940: 199).

> On every level the movement of life is through the release of energy. Psychology has shown us release and what it calls integration as one process. Social conflict is constructive when it follows this normal process, when the release of energy is by one and the same movement carrying itself to a higher level.
>
> (1924: 301)

Progress and integrating are intertwined (1924: 222, 226, 174).

> The individual is sovereign over himself as far as he unifies the heterogeneous elements of his nature. Two people are sovereign over themselves as far as they are capable of creating one out of two. A group is sovereign over itself as far as it is capable of creating one out of several or many.
>
> (Follett, 1918: 271)

Follett thus spoke of the "so-far integrated" behaviour (1924: 207) of her time: better things to come. The federalist principle at the heart of democracy would facilitate creative experience (1924: 101, 111).

Follett vividly imagined possibilities that enthralled her. She also believed that without imagination and enthusiasm, these possibilities would never have a chance to come to fruition (1924: 300–303). This frame of mind does not prevail in contemporary professional and intellectual circles, which lean more towards scepticism and even cynicism. To read Follett is an invitation to suspend if not question the attitudes that distance us from her.

Writing and publishing were crucial to Follett's creative experience. From a disciplinary standpoint, she took the classic approach of using herself as her own subject. From a more holistic point of view, her way of life was a practice of discovery and experimentation.

Context given and made: Follett's dynamic relating

Follett belongs to an Enlightenment tradition of faith in science to solve social problems and evolve a better society, a New England ethos of self-reliance and pragmatism, and a transcendentalist culture of rejoicing in the powers of imagination.

Follett took full advantage of the unique opportunity of being part of the first generation of women to attend the world's top universities and study with the top scholars. She was then mentored by and became a mentor for leading activists and reformers. Follett pursued the best use of herself, starting from uncertainty but relying on "vital modes of association" (1924: 230) to proceed. She related dynamically as though the interdependency of personal and societal crises were established fact. Her process was to "weld the generating centres of the community into cooperating creatings of new factual happenings and new awareness" (1924: 231). In concrete terms, Follett founded and led debate clubs, social centres, and placement bureaus; she mediated industrial conflicts, and she engaged dynamic relating in business (see below).

Follett interpreted several intertwined crises: (1) political crises related to the increasing scale of the federal government, which threatened local government, and the massive influx of individuals with no experience of democracy; (2) knowledge crises related to experts' and elites' making decisions without having the relevant knowledge and bearing the consequences, as well as the disciplines' lack of relevant knowledge in the first place; and (3) personal-educational crises resulting from lack of knowledge and institutions to grow the persons who could address (1) and (2) through self-direction.

Follett's life course is remarkable in that she worked intimately with scholarly and civic leaders alike, and with individuals who intermingled their scientific and civic engagements. She benefited from pioneering experiments by creative educators at the primary, secondary and collegiate levels. The leaders of her progressive secondary school, Thayer Academy, broke with the standard practice of teaching history as memorisation of facts. Thayer's faculty led a reform movement to teach history as citizenship – the cultivation of interest in, informed opinion about, and consensus on matters of urgent public concern. Follett made a strong impression on Ana Boynton Thompson, a teacher who recommended Follett to Albert Bushnell Hart of Harvard, who recommended her to colleagues at Newnham, the women's college at Cambridge. Her primary school – that is, her relationships with her teachers and fellow students – was Follett's launching pad.

The reform method taught students to think for themselves. They had to do original research and synthesise diverse sources, including their opinions, to form a solid thesis and personal conviction. They then had to defend their position in front of the teacher and their classmates. Finally, through discussion, the class developed a consensus. Follett's teachers described this as a truth-seeking exercise (Hart, 1896). Follett applied and refined this approach in her undergraduate thesis on the Speaker of the House of Representatives (Follett 1896; Hart, 1896). In her second book, she described the process of "genuine group discussion" to "discover the truth" (Follett, 1918: 209).

Upon graduating from college, Follett and her peers struggled to find a professional footing other than teaching secondary school. Among her peers, Follett was exceptional and she knew it. She had worked with the top professors in the top universities, such as Albert Bushnell Hart at Harvard and Henry Sidgwick at Oxford; they deemed her an extraordinary student. She recognised the challenge of finding a use for herself to satisfy her own expectations as well as to express her gratitude to her teachers and her appreciation of her unique circumstances (Tonn, 2003: 64). She held herself to the highest standard in meeting this ultimate test: to find the best use of herself. To complicate matters further, Follett's society was entirely unprepared for anyone of her ilk and in many respects slammed the door. A woman who graduated from Radcliffe or the Annex did not receive a diploma, limiting her prospects for advanced study and doctoral degrees. Women were not admitted to Harvard Business School.

Follett was also acutely aware of her situation in the global and historic sense. Unskilled workers were arriving from Europe en masse. Most did not speak English and were unfamiliar with the local customs, some of which were wholly at odds with their own. There was high unemployment, particularly of youths and unskilled workers. Unemployed men frequented saloons. Adolescents dropped out of school and fell into gangs and crime (for boys) and pregnancy (girls). Middle-class and upper-class women were protesting to win the vote and participate in civic and political life. Local elites organized to fight the so-called outside influences of an increasingly centralised federal government and the patronage or boss system (O'Connor, 2012: 88–94).

Follett tried a few different paths. She began by teaching secondary school using the reformed method she was immersed in. She then joined a law office and worked on a case about municipal versus private ownership of rail lines (Tonn, 2003: 112–115). Then, like many of her peers, she became active in the Settlement House Movement (SHM). The thrust of this movement was to "settle" immigrants by co-locating them in houses with resident educators and organizers who offered education, health care, child care and recreation. A key SHM principle was reciprocity: there was no "giver" and "receiver" of services; both benefited from the relationship.

Follett reworked this concept and practice in two key ways. First, she believed that the SHM's scope and efficiency were limited because it organized in private homes. Instead, she offered SHM curricula at public schools during the evenings and in the summer. Second, she believed that adolescents in particular rejected SHM programs because of their maternalism. The SHM was run by women, for women and their children. Follett believed that this discouraged young men and all adolescents. More subtly, she perceived a condescending attitude on the part of SHM leaders. The reciprocity principle was not practiced and often reverted to self-interest or even coercion. The civic groups that targeted young men, on the other hand, were led by elites who preferred to inculcate ideas by reading patriotic speeches. Follett found this practice altogether too passive and doctrinaire, and in fact contrary to the meaning of democracy.

Follett's innovation was to apply the same methods that her own teachers and peer-educators had used in order to integrate adolescents, women and immigrants into the practice of relating as a member to a society defined as a work in progress interdependent with recognising one's personally meaningful stakes in making that (his, her, our) society. She began by setting up a debate club for young second-generation Irish men, which developed into a training and mentorship program for entering local politics. She then formed five social centres throughout Boston for adult and adolescent first- and second-generation immigrants. Ostensibly, the activities were recreational and cultural, but the purpose was to cultivate self-governing capacity in individuals and communities. She organized the centres into clubs, and each one ran itself like a small business. The athletic clubs sponsored tournaments, the arts clubs gave performances, and so forth. These events generated revenues that the clubs managed for purposes that they decided for themselves. This focus on responsibility and decision-making marked the point where things got interesting for Follett (see O'Connor, 2012: 98–102).

Follett's culminating move was adding the career piece. She believed that professional vocational counsellors focused only on the short term, matching applicants to the first available job. The developmental, long-term aspect was missing. Many people, particularly young people, needed a third point of view on their job experience – not theirs and not that of their employers. Follett brought placement counsellors into the centres, who developed personal relationships with the club members and lent this perspective. Follett saw the relating between club members and counsellors as facilitating relationships across the major domains of life – economic, recreational and civic – and most importantly of all, doing so in an atmosphere free of authority relations and based on "free play".

Follett and management

As the centres she had founded won public support and funding, they were spun off to the City of Boston. Follett documented their progress in her book, *The New State* (1918). She then worked in arbitration and mediation, as shown in *Creative Experience* (1924). Through her close ties to business leaders such as retailer Edward Filene and manufacturer Henry Dennison, she became active in the movement to professionalise management.

Because Follett had immersed herself in the SHM, her reworking of the SHM and local politics, it is an understatement to say that she made a bold move when she stated that democracy was not working and that the world had failed to grasp its essential idea (Metcalf & Urwick, 1940: 94). Looking for the most creative possibility, she discovered the greatest vitality among businessmen. In particular, she observed a specific function, management, charged with executing creative experience and dynamic relating. Management is a "pivot" of interacting forces (Metcalf & Urwick, 1940: 17–19). Like Simon, she did focus on a specific setting – organization – but her interest was the interplay of forces within and around the manager that made the function boundaryless and freeing.

Business is "on the verge of making large contributions to something far more important than democracy, democracy in its more superficial meaning – to the development of integrative unity" (Metcalf & Urwick, 1940: 94). Business is an experimental laboratory to solve not only problems of organization but the hardest problems of human relations (Metcalf & Urwick, 1940: 269). Organization entails "group power" (Metcalf & Urwick, 1940: 283); its very purpose is collective creativity (1924: 130–131, 302).

Organization flourishes as it unifies internally and externally.

> The first test of business administration . . . should be whether you have a business with all its parts so coordinated, so moving together in their closely knit and adjusting activities, so linking, interlocking, interrelating, that they make a working unit.
>
> (Metcalf & Urwick, 1940: 71)

The chief executive's responsibility is "to see that all possible contributions are utilized and made into an organized, significant whole subordinated to a common purpose" (Metcalf & Urwick, 1940: 283).

> If a chief executive cannot integrate the different policies in his business, that is, if he cannot make his executives unite wholeheartedly on a certain policy, the suppressions will work underground and will be a very strong factor against the success of his business. For suppression means dissatisfaction, and that dissatisfaction will go on working underneath . . . and may crop up at any moment in some place where we least desire to see it . . . where it will give us more trouble than if we had dealt with it in the first instance.
>
> (Urwick, 1949: 68)

Problems should be solved where they arise, conflicts reconciled where conflict occurs (Metcalf & Urwick, 1940: 154).

The leader must "relate all the complex outer forces and all the complex inner forces". The leader brings to bear "a common purpose, born of the desires and the activities of the group" (Metcalf & Urwick, 1940: 260–267). The leader is able to see the whole and his or her relationship to it and articulates this view throughout. There is no personal or arbitrary element: the situation has its own authority (Metcalf & Urwick, 1940: 150). Thus the leader too obeys – the law of the situation (see below). "One man seldom knows enough about the matter in hand to impose his will on others", so resolution engages "the reciprocally modified judgment" of all concerned. The leader's task is to facilitate these processes and win such judgment (Metcalf & Urwick, 1940: 284).

The leader must help others participate in his leadership. "The best leader knows how to make his followers actually feel power themselves". Moreover, leaders need to be followers, because they create "a partnership, a joint responsibility, in a common task" (Metcalf & Urwick, 1940: 290). All organizational units – members, groups, functions, departments and so forth – are parts in the whole and must understand themselves as such. Naturally, each has its individual interest, but each must be able to integrate these interests to make the final product. "It isn't enough to do my part well and leave the matter there. I must study how my part fits into every other part and change my work if necessary so that all parts can work harmoniously and effectively together" (Urwick, 1949: 76). The subtle point is to consider one's function relative to "the good of the business as viewed from his department". It is not about balancing individual versus whole interest, but considering what is good for the whole from the vantage point of the department (Metcalf & Urwick,

1940: 73–74). Side-taking is not objectionable. What matters is whether they are self-interested sides, versus sides that see themselves as parts of a functional unity.

Follett noted the irony that although organization makes integration more necessary, it has features that block integration, notably hierarchy (chain of command and power relations) and impersonality. Concerning the former, formal organization delineates vertical positions, but there is a corresponding need for horizontal ones when "a problem which occurs at X which concerns Y does not have to be taken up the line from X and then down the line to Y". Follett called this cross-functioning. "Where you have direct contact there is much less chance of misunderstanding, there is opportunity of explaining problems and difficulties" (Urwick, 1949: 64).

On the classic problem of centralisation versus decentralisation, Follett held that both are necessary. This is precisely the trick. "I believe that collective responsibility and decentralized responsibility must go hand in hand; more than that, I think they are parts of the same thing" (Metcalf & Urwick, 1940: 79). A strong whole requires parts that integrate within themselves. It is not a matter of finding a balance between them but of having both. "This is one of our gravest problems: how to foster local initiative and at the same time get the advantages of centralization" (Metcalf & Urwick, 1940: 80). There is too much emphasis on the individual's function in the whole and not enough on one's being responsible for a functional whole (Metcalf & Urwick, 1940: 80). Each member has a double responsibility: (1) for his particular function in the whole, and (2) for his part to make a functioning whole. Individual responsibility has been discussed, but the emphasis also needs to be put on organizing such that workers, managers and owners feel a collective responsibility. The process begins with responsibility to the immediate work group and scales up. Ultimately, workers, managers, all departments and so forth have the same interests (Metcalf & Urwick, 1940: 80–81).

Executives tend to separate from workers and present policy such that co-workers "have to take a for-or-against attitude" (1924: 217). Lines between managers and workers are artificial and divisive. The idea that hourly employees do not or need not engage their full faculties reduces the creative prospects (Metcalf & Urwick, 1940: 71). The worker who decides to execute an assigned task is managing. Most people have managing ability, and they need the opportunity to exercise their ability. "We want to make use of what they have". "[W]hen men are allowed to use their own judgment in regard to the matter of executing orders, and *accept the responsibility involved in that*, then they are managing" (Metcalf & Urwick, 1940: 85–88, emphasis in original). Unions are beneficial to the extent that they encourage workers' participation in managerial functions but counterproductive when workers transfer their power to them. Unions are also harmful when they reify fixed ideas about labour and capital.

More subtly, hierarchies create the illusion that responsibility is held in some people and not in others. The "total situation" has its own impersonal and overriding authority. "One person should not give orders to another person, but both should agree to take their orders from the situation". The great potential for scientific management is depersonalisation of orders by finding the law of the situation (Metcalf & Urwick, 1940: 59).

Looking back and forward: summary and conclusion

Unless management means leading a creative life or devoting oneself to creative activity, we err in calling Follett a management theorist. She sought out and created relationships that helped her understand and embody creative relating. Her relationships with teachers and fellow students launched her on this path. In her early career, her relationships with activists and social experiments resonated. Later on, working in industry, she found that businesspeople were "more consciously and deliberately" pioneering in co-creating. Studying with them was, she said, "as thrilling an experience as going into a new country and building railroads over new mountains".

We cannot capture Follett's interior life, but she conveys the joy of being at the brink and heart of extraordinary discoveries. When she refers to "'that mystery moment' which leads from the existing to the new . . . a *progressive* experience, the way of individual and social development" (1924: xv, emphasis in original), she is describing her personal experience of (1) relating to her experience; (2) joining with others who have similar desires and building the power to achieve and evolve those desires; and (3) relating to an imminent historical and evolutionary process. Better understandings of creative relating would advance government and international relations and help solve world problems (Metcalf & Urwick, 1940: 18–19).

No single body of work takes on Follett's full scope and depth, but three rich streams that build on key aspects are Gittell's works (Gittell (2016), Gittell and Douglass (2012) and Gittel and Fletcher (2017)), Hatchuel (2005) and O'Connor (2012). Jody Gittell and her colleagues at the Relational Coordination Research Collaborative, Brandeis University, and their international community of affiliated researchers have developed theory and research founded on reciprocal relating in organizational settings. They propose a relational coordination theory of organizational performance and a relational model of organizational change. They have also built a diagnostic tool, the relational coordination survey, which captures the quantity and quality of relations in complex situations with multiple interdependent actors. Armand Hatchuel and his colleagues at MINES ParisTech establish the theoretical foundation for a science of collective action (Segrestin et al., 2017). They posit continuous reciprocity among knowledge creation, application and social relations (e.g. actors' embeddedness in organized settings). In particular, they exploit the creative possibilities for invention and innovation. Follett admitted that she asked a lot by aiming to grasp the complexity of co-creating without betraying its fundamentally dynamic nature. Hatchuel et al. live up to her ambition. O'Connor works to keep Follett's concept of management in play. She argues that elite business schools went astray when they organized management as a hybrid discipline made up of core or foundational disciplines in the social and quantitative sciences on the one hand, and applied fields such as marketing and finance on the other. This move makes it impossible for the field to have a central and unifying focus, much less a general theory and research agenda. Creative relating is the proper focus because the purpose of organization is value creation through the coordination of multiple interacting parts, and the executive takes responsibility for and works toward that purpose (Barnard, 1968 [1938]).

A more complete integration of Follett requires crossing boundaries among scientific practice, ordinary action, and philosophies and ways of life. The field has far to go in valuing and understanding the individual and agency (Suddaby et al., 2013). This entails studying the care of the self relating creatively to the care of the beyond-the-self. Ultimately, Follett proposes a theory, practice and example of the individual constructing her life in this way. Could there be a science and/or art of constructing one's life? This inquiry requires a sensibility that is at once self- and other-centred; past, present and future oriented; and scientifically, philosophically and practically grounded. Ultimately, Follett answered a call that she created in the first place. Much remains to be understood about this intimate and expansive circularity.

Recommended reading

Original text by Follett

Follett, M. (1924). *Creative experience*. New York: Longmans, Green. https://archive.org/details/creativeexperien00foll

Key academic text

O'Connor, E. (2012). *Creating new knowledge in management: Appropriating the field's lost foundations*. Stanford, CA: Stanford University Press.

Accessible resource

Tonn, J. (2003). *Mary P. Follett: Creating democracy, transforming management.*
New Haven, CT: Yale University Press.

References

Barnard, C. (1968 [1938]). *The functions of the executive.* 2nd edition. Boston: Harvard Business School Press.

Cabot, R. (1934). "Mary Parker Follett, an appreciation." *Radcliffe Quarterly*, April: 80–82.

Follett, M. (1924). *Creative experience.* New York: Longmans, Green.

Follett, M. (1918). *The new state.* New York: Longmans, Green.

Follett, M. (1896). *The speaker of the House of Representatives.* New York: Longmans, Green.

Gittell, J. (2016). *Transforming relationships for high performance: The power of relational coordination.* Stanford, CA: Stanford University Press.

Gittell, J., and Douglass, A. (2012). "Relational bureaucracy: Structuring reciprocal relationships into roles." *Academy of Management Review* 37, 4: 709–754.

Gittell, J., and Fletcher J. (2017). "Developing integrative solutions in a divided world." In Stout, M. (ed.), *The future of progressivism: Applying Follettian thinking to contemporary issues.* Claremont, CA: Process Century Press.

Hart, A. (1896). "Introduction." In Follett, M. (ed.), *The speaker of the house of representatives.* New York: Longmans, Green, pp. xi–xvi.

Hatchuel, A. (2005). "Towards an epistemology of collective action." *European Management Review* 2, 1: 36–47.

Holt, E. (1915). *The Freudian wish: The place of illusory experience in a realistic world.* New York: Henry Holt.

Kanter, R. (1995). "Preface." In Graham, P. (ed.), *Mary Parker Follett: Prophet of management: A celebration of writings from the 1920s.* Boston: Harvard Business School Press, pp. xiii–xix.

Metcalf, H., and Urwick, L. (eds.). (1940). *Dynamic administration: The collected papers of Mary Parker Follett.* New York: Harper.

Nohria, N. (1995). "Mary Parker Follett's view on power, the giving of orders, and authority: An alternative to hierarchy or a utopian ideology?" In Graham, P. (ed.), *Mary Parker Follett: Prophet of management: A celebration of writings from the 1920s.* Boston: Harvard Business School Press, pp. 154–162.

O'Connor, E. (2012). *Creating new knowledge in management: Appropriating the field's lost foundations.* Stanford, CA: Stanford University Press.

Segrestin, B., Aggeri, F., David, A., and Le Masson, P. (2017). "Armand Hatchuel and the refoundation of management research: Design theory and the epistemology of collective action." In Szabla, D., Pasmore, W., Barnes, M., and Gipson, A. (eds.), *The Palgrave handbook of organizational change thinkers.* London: Palgrave Macmillan, pp. 575–588.

Spender, J. (2013). "Herbert Alexander Simon: Philosopher of the organizational life-world." In Witzel, M., and Warner, M. (eds.), *The Oxford handbook of management theorists*. Oxford: Oxford University Press, pp. 297–360.

Suddaby, R., Foster, W., and Mills, A. (2013). "Historical institutionalism." In Bucheli, M., and Wadhwani, R. (eds.), *Organizations in time: History, theory, methods*. Oxford: Oxford University Press, pp. 100–123.

Tonn, J. (2003). *Mary P. Follett: Creating democracy, transforming management*. New Haven, CT: Yale University Press.

Urwick, L. (ed.). (1949). *Freedom & co-ordination: Lectures in business organization by Mary Parker Follett*. London: Management Publications Trust.

3   Arlie Russell Hochschild

Jenna Ward

Arlie Russell Hochschild has published over 60 articles and chapters and ten award-winning books. Her accessible and timely contributions to sociological understandings of work, family, gender and emotion distinguish her as founder of a sociology of emotion. For Hochschild, emotions are key to understanding social life: they are the all too often hidden and unspoken connection between public and private, macro and micro, visible and intimate, work and family. Yet, despite her prolific 50-year career, advocating the importance of emotions, she is most well-known and most regularly cited in the field of organization studies: emotional labour. This chapter, while paying due diligence to emotional labour and its impact on the discipline, purposefully draws on Hochschild's work beyond *The Managed Heart* to question why these works have received comparable neglect in organization studies.

The daughter of a US ambassador, Arlie Russell Hochschild grew up surrounded by difference and diplomacy. In the preface to *The Managed Heart* she recounts how, as a 12-year-old at parties hosted by her parents, she would watch the smiles of the foreign diplomats wax and wane and questioned whether she had "passed the peanuts to a person . . . or an actor?" (1983: ix). Such early childhood experiences ingrained in Hochschild an ability to question what others take for granted while igniting her interest in emotion.

After graduating from Swarthmore College in 1962 with a BA in International Relations, Hochschild pursued postgraduate education in Sociology at the University of California, Berkeley. As a graduate student she became excited by the work of C. Wright Mills, recounting how she read and re-read *White Collar* in search of an answer to the question she had been so astute to ask as a child: to whom had she passed the peanuts? Mills's observation that we have the ability to sell our personalities at the cost of self-estrangement both pleased and troubled Hochschild simultaneously. Yes, this is what she had witnessed growing up as a child in faraway lands and, indeed, went on to explore in more depth in her first academic paper in 1969 and again more recently in a chapter titled "The Diplomat's Wife" (2013). Yet, at the same time, Mills's assumption that having a personality automatically meant that it was a saleable commodity did not fit with her own experiences. Selling a personality required active selling. That sale, like all other sales, required effort in the form of labour: emotional labour.

It is for the concept of emotional labour that Arlie Russell Hochschild is best known. *The Managed Heart* catapulted Hochschild into the limelight. A concept so pervasive, tangible and recognisable presented in all of its conceptual complexity in an accessible text was irresistible to a broad spectrum of disciplines and was rightly awarded the *New York Times'* "Notable Social Science Book of the Year" (1983).

Despite the success of *The Managed Heart*, however, the married mother of two boys continued to develop her thinking on emotion beyond the concept of emotional labour. For Hochschild, emotion is a sense, like seeing and hearing: "it is through emotion that we know the world" (2013:4). It is this fundamental premise that defines what has been referred to as *Hochschildian Sociology* (Wharton, 2011). A form of sociological enquiry that "reflects a concern with families, children and what might still be referred to as private life" (2011: 463), that focuses attention on the nature of human relationships and the networks of obligation, emotion and care that bind people together – both in public and private, and advocates a commitment to understanding how the personal, private and familial realms have been and continue to be encroached on and invariably altered by powerful, inflexible institutions such as the workplace. For me, then, a Hochschildian sociology is characterised by an emotionally focused, palpably sensitive exploration of the uneasy work-family symbiosis.

While her subsequent works on the broader emotional system, work-family life, global care chains and the impact of the neoliberal agenda on intimate life has generated more than 60 papers, ten sociological books, four honorary doctorates and endorsement by the American Sociological Association as one of the leading feminist sociologists of the last 30 years, very little of her work beyond the concept of emotional labour has made its way into organization and management studies. This chapter serves to illustrate what we as organization scholars have been missing out on in the past 30 years and implicitly to question why her work beyond *The Managed Heart* has been neglected by scholars of organization and management. I begin with an overview of Hochschild's seminal work on emotional labour, emotion management and feeling rules to explore the boundaries between public and private emotion, before moving on to review a much broader body of work spanning the 30 years between 1983 and 2013, in which Hochschild's work became focused on the work-family boundary negotiations and in particular the emotional and social impacts on and of care. I conclude with her more recent and compelling thoughts on empathy maps and their potential for application to understanding conflict and resistance in organizational contexts.

The Managed Heart

Publication of *The Managed Heart* (1983) stimulated a "tremendous amount of research" (Wharton, 2009: 147) exploring the ways in which we manage our emotions and feelings in various contexts. The accessibility, timeliness and acute resonance of the issues raised within the text inspired a generation of scholars, myself included, across a breadth of disciplines, not least those engaged with the study of organizations and management. However, Hochschild's work is often used as a springboard for departure rather than a wellspring for sustenance, which is cited rather than draws upon or attends to the original text (Kruml & Geddes, 2000). The resulting "bandwagon" phenomenon (Bolton, 2005) or "semantic morass" (McClure & Murphy, 2008: 105), while rapidly developing the sub-field of work-based studies of emotion and in many ways enriching our knowledge of emotions at work, also produced conflicting and contending perspectives as well as both popular and neglected areas of study (McClure & Murphy, 2008; Callahan & McCollum, 2002). Today, you would be hard-pressed to find an academic of management studies who did not think themselves familiar with the concepts of emotional labour, emotion management and emotion work. Everyone, it seems, has heard of *The Managed Heart*, even if they have not read it.

The proliferation of secondary interpretations of the core concepts introduced in *The Managed Heart*, however, often obscures Hochschild's original construction of the terms and, for me, perhaps more importantly the heritage from which these ideas were borne. Emotional labour is not a vacuous construct bereft of a conceptual, ontological and theoretical legacy. Instead it is the culmination of over a decade of "figuring out" (Hochschild in Kimmel, 2015) and the cornerstone of, what has become known as a Hochschildian sociology. In the interests of clarification, I take Hochschild (1983) as both a starting point and a referent throughout this chapter.

From Hochschild's (1975, 1979, 1983, 1989a) perspective, emotional labour arises from the rational commodification of emotions. Presenting work-based narratives from both airborne cabin crew and land-based debt collectors, *The Managed Heart* demonstrated ways in which the terms physical and mental labour did not adequately describe the work undertaken in these job roles. Hochschild convincingly presented the argument that employee emotions had become subject to managerial remote control; that both the men and women she interviewed and observed were, in effect, selling an emotional part of their selves to their employing organizations in exchange for a wage, in much the same way as physical labour power had been understood to be commodified since Marx. She accordingly deployed the term "emotional labour" to designate

> the management of feeling to create a publicly observable facial and bodily display; emotional labour is sold for a wage and therefore has *exchange-value*. . . . This labour requires one to induce or suppress feeling in order to sustain the outward countenance that produces the proper state of mind in others.
>
> (Hochschild, 1983:7, emphasis in original)

As a sociologist Hochschild self-identified the origin of her thoughts on emotional labour as being in her reading of Marx. Though this has been disputed (see Bolton, 2009, and in defence of Hochschild, Brook, 2009), she herself contends that organizations commodify individuals' emotions in return for a wage to the extent that particular emotions come to have "exchange-value". This process of commodification is seen by Hochschild to be in line with Marx's depiction of the labour process as exploitative in terms of the capitalist extraction and accumulation of surplus value, recognising the potentially negative effects on the psychological and physical health and well-being of those performing emotional labour in exchange for a wage. Hochschild, aware of the potential limitations of her carefully selected contrasting empirical samples, encouraged further research into the effects (and varieties) of emotional labour and modestly suggested that *The Managed Heart* aimed only to "introduce the concept of 'emotional labour' and 'feeling rules' (the norms which govern emotional labour), and the 'emotional exchanges' on which these bear" (Hochschild, 1989a: 441).

Neo-functionalists were energised by the concept of feeling rules, emphasising the rule-governed aspect; human capital economists warmed to the transactional approach toward emotions; and labour process researchers saw it as an extension to the new vocabularies of (de-)skilling, control and resistance that they had been developing post-Braverman (1974). Yet much of this work interpreted the emotional labour thesis pessimistically (Wouters, 1989a; 1989b). Consequently, between 1983 and 1989 both the psychological and sociological literature focused attention on the negative consequences of performing emotional labour. Burnout, emotional exhaustion, alienation, depersonalisation, stress, depression and self-estrangement were all offered as potential consequences of emotional labour (Hochschild, 1983; Ashforth & Humphrey, 1993; Ashforth & Tomuik, 2000). The commodification of private emotions and sentiments was argued to leave the individual with an unstable self-identity, a secondary ontological insecurity, unsure of whom they were, *"estranged or alienated from an aspect of self"* (Hochschild, 1983: 7). Much, but not all, of the psychological literature on emotional labour still retains this focus, establishing relationships between the performance of (different types of) emotional labour and its (various) consequences for subjective well-being, job satisfaction and even physical health (Bolton 2010: 207–208; Holman et al., 2008; Mesmer-Magnus et al., 2012).

Hochschild has, however, denied any *necessary* emphasis on the damaging and alienating consequences of performing emotional labour at the cost of understanding these performances as complex emotional interactions. It is not difficult to deduce the origins of such an emphasis, given that her seminal text opens with a quote from C. Wright Mills and a comparative example with Marx. Launching a critique on these grounds, Wouters claimed that Hochschild's "preoccupation with the 'costs' of emotion work not only leads to a one-sided and moralistic interpretation of the working conditions of flight attendants, it also hampers understanding the joy the job may bring" (1989a: 116). Hochschild responded that her drawing on Marx was to focus attention on the changing nature of constraints on workers rather than on the quantity of those constraints and their associated outcomes. Social constraints upon workers are increasingly aimed at an individual internal level, she argued, as "we are controlled to a greater extent through our feelings, and less through our externally observable behaviour" (Hochschild, 1989b: 442). More recently, Hochschild has returned to these issues in a discursive chapter titled "Can Emotional Labour Be Fun?" and in an article in the *International Journal of Work, Organization and Emotion* (2009) of the same name, in which she argues that while "one can enjoy emotional labour immensely . . . provided one has an affinity for it and a workplace that supports that affinity" (2013: 25), the contemporary reality of this type of work and the employment contexts in which it is often carried out sets a "tragic cycle in motion" (2013: 30). A cycle in which one might take great pride in caring for others through emotional labour performances but the organizations in which this work is carried out demonstrates very little by way of care for those employees (Smith, 2012). Being required to care by those who show little compassion, on low-pay, zero-hour contracts and in highly bureaucratised systems leaves emotional labourers disheartened and detached from their work, leading Hochschild to ask, "Who takes care of the caretaker?" (2004). It is important to remember, that despite the cross-disciplinary success of *The Managed Heart*, it needs to be read and understood as a product of Hochschild's sociology of emotion and her socio-political view of the current state of care, iconically summarised in *The Commercialisation of Intimate Life*: "Ideologically, 'care' went to heaven. Practically, it's gone to hell" (Hochschild, 2003: 2).

The Hochschild and Wouters debate (Wouters, 1989a, 1989b; Hochschild, 1989b) arguably marked the point of departure between the sociology of work and work psychology's treatments of emotional labour. Much of the sociological literature began to reconsider the effects of the labour and came to focus on identifying a range of job roles that required the management of emotions, while work psychology continued to pursue evidence of causal relationships between emotional labour performances and their impact on job satisfaction and individual well-being.

Sociological research interests (incorporating those of organizational behaviour and nursing) subsequently bifurcated. The first branch focused on emotional labour as a distinctive feature of particular occupations, with examples varying from flight attendants (Tyler & Taylor, 2001; Williams, 2003) and nurses (Bolton, 2000, 2005; Theodosius, 2008) to bus drivers (Scott & Barnes, 2011; Scott et al., 2012) and even academics (Ogbonna & Harris, 2004). Within this branch, in Europe in particular, many authors were influenced by developments in labour process theory and more recently Italian autonomism, with express interest in how emotions were controlled and used to control workplace subjectivity, but also how they might be a resource for resistance to commodification (Vincent, 2011). Consequently, sociological discussions in this area attempt to maintain a clear distinction between Hochschild's original definitions of emotional labour, emotion work and emotion management. Emotional labour is the management of emotion that has exchange value and therefore takes place within a public context as part of an employment relationship. Emotion work (and emotion management, as in Hochschid's original definition) is the management of feeling in a private context that has use value. Over time, the term emotion management has come to be used as an umbrella term for both emotional labour and emotion work, particularly where a clear distinction is not evident – a problem Bolton (2010) sought to redress with her typology of emotion management.

The second branch of sociology of work research has focused on the emotions themselves and worker attempts to manage them. Most significant is the work on display and feeling rules that govern the nature, depth and experience of emotion management. The flight attendants Hochschild observed and interviewed spent their days working to suppress their own feelings of exhaustion, frustration and fear while simultaneously enacting emotions to create a cheerful, carefree pleasurable experience for their passengers in line with the regulations prescribed by the airline. Positive interpersonal interactions such as this can be understood to be a product of the expression of *integrative* emotions (Diefendorff et al., 2006) or the performance of *positive* (Rafaeli & Sutton, 1987) or *empathetic* (Korczynski, 2003) emotional labour.

The bill collectors, whose emotion management was compared with that of the flight attendants, undertook work that required them to induce fear, surprise and intimidation in their clients. Such negative service interactions (from the client's perspective) can be seen to entail *differentiating* emotions (Diefendorff et al., 2006) or the performance of *negative* (Rafaeli & Sutton, 1987) or *antipathetic* (Korczynski, 2003) emotional labour. Thus, the roles of flight attendant and bill collector are presented as involving antipathetic emotion management practices. However, Ward and McMurray (2011: 1585) argue that these dichotomous conceptualisations of emotional labour overlook job roles that require the suppression of felt emotions while "displaying unemotional behaviour, wherein the suppression of the emotion is the performance itself", which they define as *emotional neutrality*. Emotional neutrality has identified as an important part of the emotional labour repertoire of general practitioner receptionists (Ward & McMurray, 2011) and call centre workers (Bunting, 2004).

Such conceptual distinctions are being made, then, on the type of emotion displayed during emotional labour performances. Despite *The Managed Heart* presenting a comparison of job roles characterised by empathetic and antipathetic performances, the studies it has inspired have almost exclusively focused on roles characterised by positive emotional performances thereby marginalising the nature of the emotional labour required by those employed to enact much darker, more uncomfortable and often unspoken work. In 2016, Ward and McMurray's text *The Dark Side of Emotional Labour* shined a spotlight into darker corners of work and occupational roles where feelings are commodified not to make customers feel happy, content or cared for but instead to scare, threaten or intimidate. This text was written in an attempt to redress the asymmetry in the extant organization studies literatures, in which empirical contexts for studying emotional labour are such that, whether purposeful or otherwise, emotional labour is frequently and consistently presented as low-skilled, low-paid women's work.

Not only did Hochschild introduce us to different types of emotions induced via performances of emotional labour, but she also conceptualised two methods by which this is often achieved on the part of the emotional labourer. Derived from Goffman (1959), *surface acting* involves managing outward appearances; pretending "to feel what we do not, . . . we deceive others about what we really feel, but we do not deceive ourselves" (Hochschild, 1983: 33). In this case, the emotional labourer is able to articulate the difference between what they genuinely feel and the impression they are projecting. Put simply, surface acting is the art of impression management, which involves "stimulating emotions that are not actually felt, which is accomplished by careful presentation of verbal and nonverbal cues, such as facial expression, gestures, and voice tone" (Ashforth & Humphrey, 1993: 91).

Deep acting, on the other hand, is the act of "deceiving oneself as much as deceiving others . . . we make feigning easy by making it unnecessary" (Hochschild, 1983: 33). Deep acting is seen to entail a successful transmutation of the private emotional system, as the emotional labourer begins to feel that the normative requirements prescribed by the organization are, in fact, their own. In such cases, then, behavioural change is an indirect consequence of deep acting, for it is inner feelings that are being manipulated directly, not outward manifestations of those emotions. Deep acting has been associated with less obvious negative effects than surface acting (Hochschild, 1983; Bono & Vey, 2005; Scott & Barnes, 2011). However, Hochschild, and those who see emotional labour as an extension of the labour process, would argue that the successful transmutation of the private emotional system is the ultimate in capitalist subordination.

A third, and often overlooked, form of emotion management is the *expression of genuinely felt emotions* (Ashforth & Humphrey, 1993) or *automatic emotion regulation* (Zapf, 2002). Hochschild's (1983) conceptualisation of emotion management implies that all emotions have to be consciously managed. However, Ashforth and Humphrey (1993: 93) argue that this conceptualisation of emotional labour "does not allow for instances whereby one spontaneously and genuinely experiences and expresses the expected emotion".

Interestingly, during my own doctoral research (2009) I observed how the training delivered by budget airlines to cabin crew in the UK did not specify any requirement to manage their emotions or those of passengers. In effect, there were no explicit feeling rules to follow, as this facet of the training had been eliminated through cost cutting. However, this did not translate into cabin behaviours that were broadly any different to those observed by Hochschild and others who have studied the emotional labour of flight attendants (Tyler & Abbott, 1998; Taylor & Tyler, 2000). Instead, I argued that budget airlines rely on organizational feeling rules being replaced by social norms and expectations of the job role synonymous with those expected by full-service-provider airlines. Bolton (2010: 213) sees this sort of dynamic extending even further to the demands of society rather than the demands of capital. Diefendorff et al. (2006: 273), along with others, see display rules as "unwritten norms", and Zapf refers to these as "implicit emotional display rules", arguing they become known through "high performance expectations" (2002: 241).

For Rafaeli and Sutton (1987), role expectations are created, influenced and maintained by the organizational context (recruitment and selection, socialisation and rewards and punishments) and emotional transactions. The actual emotional transaction that takes place with the customer, or more generally the service recipient, will govern the emotional display. This is because society and the market are indoctrinated with role expectations about the service they should receive during an interaction. In addition, their emotional tone is also governed by societies' expectations of them as customers. These complex relationships construct the identities of both the customer and the front-line representative, as self and "other", simultaneously, as both parties uphold role expectations. Often there is a dominant expectation that a professional and rational self is emotion-free, predicated on the idea that emotion gets in the way of rational understanding (Hochschild, 2013: 4). For those of us who identify as Hochschildian sociologists – or at least sociologists of emotion, inspired by Hochschild's way of seeing – this fundamental premise is highly problematic. Yet it is important to note that all of these debates stem from her original and continuing work. Indeed, adopting an emotions lens offers an alternative reading of the boundaries between work and home, policy and micro-experience, care and convenience. It is to these everyday intersections that Hochschild's work, after *The Managed Heart*, attends.

A broken care system

In 1989, just six years after *The Managed Heart*, *The Second Shift* was published. Now, while *The Managed Heart* had seen Hochschild catapulted to centre stage in management and organization studies and beyond, her new, equally poignant and highly critical account of the human impact of the work-family balance on two-career couples received considerably less attention in this field. Indeed, even today, Hochschild's works beyond *The Managed Heart* are largely invisible in management and organization studies. This is not an issue of quality, however, for *The Second Shift* received just as much critical acclaim as *The Managed Heart*, similarly being identified as a *New York Times* "Notable Social Science Book of the Year" (1989). It is worthwhile, therefore, presenting an overview of Hochschild's post-*The Managed Heart* portfolio, as it has much to offer organization and management scholars.

The Second Shift, published by Penguin in 1989 and since translated into five other languages, placed a sharp focus on the stresses and strains predominantly experienced by working women in relation to the proportion, character and quality of family life tasks for which they are responsible. The term "the second shift" poignantly reflects the multiplicity of responsibilities and tasks undertaken by women in addition to their paid work. The washing, cooking, organizing homework, co-ordinating after school activities and caring for ailing parents are in and of themselves full-time jobs, and yet they are undertaken by most without payment. They are more often than not tasks either undertaken or at least co-ordinated by women. The work of the 1950s housewife has not disappeared, but it has become increasingly invisible, pushed further back in the day, rarely spoken about, absorbed by women and families as they battle against structural pressures such as the increasing precarity of work and a continuous erosion of the welfare state. Hochschild's point remains then, that undertaking the second shift comes at a cost, sometimes physically but almost always emotionally.

The Time Bind (1997) saw a combination of the social issues documented in *The Second Shift* and the emotional experiences and coping strategies employed by parents and workers to cope with work and family demands in an existence dominated by time. Having spent 3 years interviewing and observing employees of a Fortune 500 company in the United States, Hochschild presents the emotional costs of contemporary work. The guilt, anxiety and inadequacies felt by parents and partners are portrayed vividly: men feeling inadequate as fathers because they struggle to find regular work; women feeling guilty for buying shop-made cupcakes for their sons to take to the school bake sale; children attempting to cash in on their parents' perceived deficits to get what they want. Here then, we see the introduction of the "third shift": the emotion management of coping with a lack of time; the negotiating, reconciling and resisting just to make time to work and live.

The Outsourced Self: Intimate Life in Market Times (2012) observes the ways in which market forces and the associated structural pressures of capitalism both create the time bind but also offer "solutions". This text explores the growing trend to pay for personal services that previously we would have attended to personally. Examples include paying someone to clean your house, look after your children, plan your wedding, or (in the extreme) have a baby on your behalf.

Indeed, both *The Commercialisation of Intimate Life* (2003) and "*So, How's the Family?*" (2013) perhaps best express Hochschild's current conceptual project. In particular, "*So How's the Family?*" a collection of short essays, collectively explores the ways in which neoliberal public policy comes home to add to "the second (and therefore, third) shift" (e.g. unregulated junk food advertising increasing child obesity leads to parents (often mothers) having to make more trips to the doctors, further adding to the "time bind"). This, then, is the overarching narrative of Hochschild's sociology of emotion. Barbara Ehrenreich wrote that "Arlie is one of the great, even iconic social thinkers of our time . . . her work is informed by dazzling intellect and deep moral passion" (2011), and this intellectual project that has spanned her 50-year career is testament to that.

Hochschild's ability to insightfully link macro-, meso- and micro-experiences in a voice imbued with compassion is what makes her one of the leading social thinkers of our time. Evident in her more recent endeavours, to document how this interconnected emotional system plays out on a global scale, she gives voice to those working as part of a global nanny chain and the women who work as commercial surrogates in India. Her work speaks with a poignancy and palpably empathetic voice for those, mostly women, engaged in some of the world's most difficult and otherwise unspoken practices. These practices are evidence of a broken care system consequent of the continued pursuit of Weberian rationality and a consistent denial and active writing out of the importance of emotion in both organizational and social life.

Conclusion

Despite Arlie Russell Hochschild writing prolifically on the sociology of emotion for the past 50 years, organization and management studies have been captivated by emotional labour. While *The Managed Heart* (1983) won the *New York Times* "Notable Social Science Book of the Year" (1983), the Charles Cooley Award and the C. Wright Mills Award, it marked just the beginning of her career. It is useful to consider, then, why organization studies has become so preoccupied with *The Managed Heart* and emotional labour, leading to the comparative neglect of her publications which came to follow.

The reasons for this are perhaps twofold; first, the work that followed *The Managed Heart* was arguably "beyond rationality". Emotional labour is fundamentally the rational commodification of emotion, and therefore very clearly has instrumental and functional appeal to those interested in "managing emotions" in organizational contexts. Indeed, as was highlighted earlier, much of the focus on emotional labour was designed to determine the consequences of such performances on employees, their motivation and other job-related factors. Beyond emotional labour, then, Hochschild's work takes a more critical sociological view of the denial and subjugation of feelings, women's careers and emotional well-being, the precedence of care and family dynamics. This tranche of work forces us to ask robust questions about the very intimate impacts of social and political policies and the increasingly neoliberal market trajectories on our everyday lives, familial routines, relationships and feelings. Her work gives a voice to those who are often denied a platform to speak of their micro-experiences – those made to feel threatened, scared or without value but who are continually asked to "care" for others. It islittle wonder, then, why management and organization studies have found Hochschild's broader sociological agenda difficult to integrate.

Second, Hochschild's name has, rightly so, become synonymous with the emotional labour thesis. At the same time, emotional labour has not so rightly become gendered by the field. What I mean by this is that despite *The Managed Heart*, offering examples of both men and women performing emotional labour and different emotions (both positive and negative) being performed as part of those performances, there has been an asymmetrically gendered legacy of the text and construct. Emotional labour has been implicitly positioned as low-skilled, often low-paid women's work in management studies (see Tyler & Abbott (1998) and Taylor & Tyler (2000) for a discussion; noteworthy exceptions include Fineman and Sturdy (1999) examination of the role of emotional control for male managers and Iszatt-White (2009) consideration of the role of emotional labour in relation to effective leadership). More critical debates around emotional labour in the fields of organization studies and critical management studies have, however, developed in two directions. There are those interested in understanding emotional labour's impact on work, workers and the qualitative nature of the labour experienced in a variety of occupational contexts (see Vincent, 2011; Thompson & Smith, 2009; Williams, 2003), while others have considered emotional labour part of a wider thesis on embodiment and affect (see Hancock et al., 2015; Thanem & Knights, 2005; Witz et al., 2003; Mirchandani, 2003).

So, where next? What can organization studies learn from post-*Managed Heart* Hochschild? For those in need of inspiration for rethinking societies with significant care deficits, *"So, How's the Family?" And Other Essays* (2013) is a wellspring of ideas that places emotion and feeling firmly at their core. From empathy maps, emotional logics and relational obligations, Hochschild's ideas are ripe for investigation and application. Her endeavour, then, is to place feeling at the centre of what we do, to apply an emotions lens (2009) to help us understand how we behave and how we organize. For example, empathy maps offer a way of extending our lines of empathy, to help us reflect on the implications of our decisions and behaviours on others. In this way they have the potential to offer new ways of understanding conflict and resistance in organization, but we, as a discipline, must resist our temptation to instrumentalize these ideas and commodify them, for "empathy maps are not given to us: we [must] develop the art of making them" (Hochschild, 2013: 38) and move beyond rationality.

Recommended reading

Original text by Hochschild

Hochschild, A. R. (1983) *The Managed Heart*, Berkeley: University of California Press.

34   *Jenna Ward*

Key academic text

Wharton, A. (2009) The Sociology of Emotional Labour. *Annual Review of Sociology*, 35: 147–165.

Accessible resource

Hochschild, A. R. (1989) *The Second Shift*, New York: Penguin Books.

References

Ashforth, R. and Humphrey, B. (1993) Emotional Labour in Service Roles: The Influence of Identity. *Academy of Management Review*, 18(1): 88–118.
Ashforth, B. E. and Tomuik, M. A. (2000) Emotional Labour and Authenticity: Views from Service Agents. In S. Fineman (Ed.) *Emotions in Organizations* (2nd ed.), London: Sage.
Bolton, S. C. (2000) Who Cares? Offering Emotion Work as a 'Gift' in the Nursing Labour Process. *Journal of Advanced Nursing*, 32: 580–586.
Bolton, S. C. (2005) *Emotion Management in the Workplace*, Basingstoke: Palgrave Macmillan.
Bolton, S. C. (2009) Getting to the Heart of the Emotional Labour Process: A Reply to Brook. *Work, Employment and Society*, 23(3): 549–560.
Bolton, S. C. (2010) Old Ambiguities and New Developments: Exploring the Emotional Labour Process in Thompson, P. and Smith, C. eds. *Working Life; Renewing Labour Process Analysis*, London: Palgrave Macmillan, pp. 205–222.
Bono, J. E. and Vey, M. A. (2005) Toward Understanding Emotional Management at Work: A Qualitative Review of Emotional Labour Research. In C. E. Hartel, W. J. Zerbe and N. M. Ashkanasy (Eds.) *Emotions in Organisational Behaviour*, Mahwah, NJ: Erlbaum, pp. 213–223.
Braverman, H. (1974) *Labour and Monopoly Capital: The degradation of work in the Twentieth Century*, London: Monthly Review Press.
Brook, P. (2009) In Critical Defence of Emotional Labour: Refuting Bolton's Critique of Hochschild's Concept, *Work, Employment & Society*, 23(3): 531–548.
Bunting, M. (2004) *Willing Slaves*, London: HarperCollins.
Callahan, J. L. and McCollum, E. E. (2002) Obscured Variability: The Distinction between Emotion Work and Emotional Labour. In N. Ashkanasy, W. J. Zerbe and C. Hartel (Eds.) *Managing Emotions in the Workplace*, New York: M. E. Sharpe.
Diefendorff, J. M., Richard, E. M. and Croyle, M. H. (2006) Are Emotional Display Rules Formal Job Requirements? Examination of Employee and Supervisor Perceptions. *Journal of Occupational and Organizational Psychology*, 79: 273–298.
Ehrenreich, B. (2011) Foreword. In A. I. Garey and K. V. Hansen (Eds.) *At the Heart of Work and Family: Engaging the Ideas of Work Arlie Hochschild*, New Brunswick: Rutgers University Press, pp. xi–xii.
Fineman, S. and Sturdy, A. (1999) The Emotions of Control. *Human Relations*, 52(5): 631–663.

Goffman, E. (1959) *The Presentation of Self in Everyday Life*, London: Penguin Books.

Hancock, P., Sullivan, K., & Tyler, M. (2015) A Touch Too Much: Negotiating Masculinity, Propriety and Proximity in Intimate Labour. *Organization Studies*, 36(12): 1715–1739.

Hochschild, A. R. (1975) The Sociology of Feeling and Emotion: Selected Possibilities. *American Journal of Sociology*, 45: 2–3.

Hochschild, A. R. (1979) Emotion Work, Feeling Rules and Social Structure. *American Journal of Sociology*, 85(3): 551–575.

Hochschild, A. R. (1983) *The Managed Heart*, Berkeley: University of California Press.

Hochschild, A. R. (1989a) *The Second Shift*, New York: Penguin Books.

Hochschild, A.R. (1989b) Reply to Cas Wouter's Review Essay on the Managed Heart. *Theory, Culture and Society*, 6: 439–445.

Hochschild, A. R. (1997) *The Time Bind*, New York: Metropolitan Books.

Hochschild, A. R. (2003) *The Commercialisation of Intimate Life: Notes from Home and Work*, Berkeley: University of California.

Hochschild, A. R. (2004) Emotional Labour in Health Care: Who Takes Care of the Caretaker? In L. Dube, G. Ferland and D. S. Moskowitz (Eds.) *Enriching the Art of Care with the Science of Care; Emotional and Interpersonal Dimensions of Health Services*, Montreal: McGill Queen's University Press.

Hochschild, A. R. (2009) Can Emotional Labour be Fun? *International Journal of Work, Organization and Emotion*, 3(2).

Hochschild, A.R. (2012) *The Outsourced Self: Intimate Life in Market Times*, Picador: London.

Hochschild, A. R. (2013) *'So, How's the Family?' and Other Essays*, Berkeley: University of California Press.

Holman, D., Martinez-Inigo, D. and Totterdell, P. (2008) Emotional Labour and Employee Well-Being an Integrative View. In Ashkanasy, N and Cooper, C. L. (Eds.) *Research Companion to Emotions in Organisations*, Cheltenham: Edward Elgar, pp. 301–315.

Iszatt-White, M. (2009) Leadership as Emotional Labour: The Effortful Accomplishment of Valuing Practices. *Leadership*, 5(4): 447–467.

Korczynski, M. (2003) Communities of Coping: Collective Emotional Labour in Service Work. *Organization*, 10(1): 55–79.

Kruml, S.M. and Geddes, D. (2000) Exploring the Dimensions of Emotional Labor the Heart of Hochschild's Work. *Management Communication Quarterly*, 14(1): 8–49.

McClure, R. and Murphy, C. (2008) Contesting the Dominance of Emotional Labour in Professional Nursing. *Journal of Health Organization and Management*, 21(2): 101–120.

Mesmer-Magnus, J. R., DeChurch, L. A. and Wax, A. (2012) Moving Emotional Labour beyond Surface and Deep Acting: A Discordance-Congruence Perspective. *Organisational Psychology Review*, 2(1): 6–53.

Mirchandani, K. (2003) Challenging Racial Silences in Studies of Emotion Work: Contributions from Anti-Racist Feminist Theory. *Organization Studies*, 24(5): 721–742.

Ogbonna, E. and Harris, L. C. (2004) Work Intensification and Emotional Labour among UK University Lecturers: An Exploratory Study. *Organization Studies*, 25: 1185–1203.

Rafaeli, A., & Sutton, R. I. (1987) Expression of Emotion as Part of the Work Role. *Academy of Management Review*, 12(1): 23–37.

Scott, B. A. and Barnes, C. M. (2011) A Multilevel Field Investigation of Emotional Labor, affect, Work Withdrawal, and Gender. *Academy of Management Journal*, 54(1): 116–136.

Scott, B. A., Barnes, C. M. and Wagner, D. T. (2012) Chameleonic or Consistent? A Multilevel Investigation of Emotional Labour Variability and Self-Monitoring. *Academy of Management Journal*, 55(4): 905–926.

Smith, P. (2012) *Emotional Labour of Nursing*, Hampshire: Palgrave Macmillan.

Taylor, S. and Tyler, M. (2000) Emotional Labour and Sexual Difference in the Airline Industry. *Work, Employment & Society*, 14(1): 77–95.

Thanem, T. and Knights, D. (2005) Embodying Emotional Labour. In B. Brandeth, E. Kvande and D. Morgan (Eds.) *Gender, Bodies and Work*, Aldershot: Ashgate.

Theodosius, C. (2008) *Emotional Labour in Health Care*, London: Routledge.

Thompson, P. and Smith, C. (2009) Labour Power and Labour Process: Contesting the Marginality of the Sociology of Work. *Sociology*, 43(5): 913–930.

Tyler, M. and Abbott, P. (1998) Chocs Away: Weight Watching in the Contemporary Airline Industry. *Sociology*, 32(3): 433–450.

Tyler, M. and Taylor, S. (2001) Juggling Justice and Care: Gendered Customer Service in the Contemporary Airline Industry. In A. Sturdy, I. Grugulis, and H. Willmott (Eds.) *Customer Service: Empowerment and Entrapment*. London: Palgrave.

Vincent, S. (2011) The Emotional Labour Process: An Essay on the Economy of Feelings. *Human Relations*, 64(10): 1369–1392.

Ward, J. and McMurray, R. (2011) The Unspoken Work of General Practitioner Receptionists: A Re-Examination of Emotion Management in Primary Care. *Social Science & Medicine*, 72(10): 1583–1587.

Ward, J. and McMurray, R. (2016) *The Dark Side of Emotional Labour*, Abingdon: Routledge.

Wharton, A. (2009) The Sociology of Emotional Labour. *Annual Review of Sociology*, 35: 147–165.

Wharton, A. S. (2011) The Sociology of Arlie Hochschild. *Work and Occupations*, 38(4): 459–464.

Williams, C. (2003) Sky Service: The Demands of Emotional Labour in the Airline Industry. *Gender, Work and Organization*, 10: 513–550.

Witz, A., Warhurst, C. and Nickson, D. (2003) The Labour of Aesthetics and the Aesthetics of Organization. *Organization*, 10(1), 33–54.

Wouters, C. (1989a) The Sociology of Emotions and Flight Attendants: Hochschild's Managed Heart. *Theory, Culture & Society*, 6: 95–123.

Wouters, C. (1989b) Response to Hochschild's Reply. *Theory, Culture & Society*, 6: 447–450.

Zapf, D. (2002) Emotion Work and Psychological Well-Being: ÓA Review of the Literature and Some Conceptual Considerations. *Human Resource Management Review*, 12: 237–268.

4   Lillian Moller Gilbreth

Scott Lawley and Valerie Caven

This chapter celebrates Lillian Moller Gilbreth's[1] pioneering, foundational contributions to management theory and practice. These achievements go beyond the widely known motion study work with her husband, Frank Bunker Gilbreth, and extend to her fusion of scientific management with psychology, which foresaw human relations and behavioural approaches to management (Stead, 1974) and pre-empted many contemporary management methods and concerns such as ergonomics, personality testing and work-life balance. In later life she applied these insights to women's domestic, consumption and workplace experiences. Her career, from university to retirement in her eighties, encompassed a string of publications, awards, academic appointments, consultancies with major companies, addresses at international conferences and service on US government committees.[2] This included many "firsts", and not just as a woman. For example, her PhD from Brown University was the first psychology doctorate awarded to a woman, the first doctorate awarded in industrial psychology and the first awarded to a practitioner of scientific management (Vasquez, 2007; Lancaster, 2004; Miller and Lemons, 1998; Perloff and Naman, 1996).

Gilbreth's achievements are also remarkable given early 20th-century gender norms. She had to break new ground in areas such as academia and industrial engineering, where women faced considerable discrimination and exclusion. The recognition of her contributions is still often marginalised and overlooked, with the adjunct "and Lillian", placing her in the shadow of her husband, Frank. Furthermore, a survey of the American Academy of Management (Wren and Hay, 1977) placed Lillian behind Frank in terms of influence and the Gilbreths collectively behind other scientific management pioneers such as Frederick Taylor. A later replication of the survey (Heames and Breland, 2010) found both Gilbreths missing from the list, now also populated by human relations pioneers, such as Elton Mayo, for whom Lillian's work had paved the way. This lack of recognition is compounded by a tendency to trivialise her later work in domestic settings. The book *Cheaper by the Dozen* (Gilbreth and Carey, 1949) and subsequent Hollywood films present a quaint account of Gilbreth family life, emphasising Lillian in a homemaking role with their 12 children while playing down her professional contributions to the family business (Lancaster, 2004: 330).

Gilbreth's early life and education typifies the contradictory positions whereby she broke new ground as a woman while being constrained by gendered expectations and norms, a "struggle to attain recognition as a mother *and* career woman in a man's world". (Wren, 1972). Her well-to-do, middle-class family expected her to become a homemaker rather than enter employment. She defied expectations and attended university, where she excelled despite hostility to her presence as a woman and subtle pressures to study English because it would lead to a "feminine" career such as teaching (Vasquez, 2007; Lancaster, 2004; Miller and Lemons, 1998). One professor refused to teach women, which pushed her graduate studies towards psychology. By the time she had received her PhD at Berkeley, she had met and married Frank and had five children. These caring responsibilities were incompatible with university residential requirements, so Gilbreth was unable to receive her doctorate. Instead, she completed a second doctorate at Brown University (Perloff and Naman, 1996: 109). Frank negotiated publication of Lillian's unrewarded PhD thesis as *The Psychology of Management* (Gilbreth, 1914), with Lillian credited only as "L. M. Gilbreth". While Gilbreth broke ground as a woman publishing when this type of activity was "regarded as unsuited to members of her sex" (Mees, 2013: 39), her gender was erased due to publishers' concerns about women lacking credibility (Mees, 2013, Lancaster, 2004; Stead, 1974).

The marriage was strong and mutually beneficial – unusual at the time for having two working partners (Vasquez, 2007: 52). Frank, a pre-eminent motion study pioneer in the construction industry, used his background to further Lillian's career while developing his own work by drawing upon her psychological insights. Again, there was a contradiction that, while Lillian broke ground as a woman, the marriage replicated gender norms, with Lillian conforming to traditional roles within the relationship by taking on domestic and family responsibilities (Miller and Lemons, 1998: 6). Professionally, she existed in Frank's shadow as his "apprentice and partner" (Vasquez, 2007: 52), casting herself as "promoter" or "assistant" (Mees, 2013; Miller and Lemons, 1998) despite making an equal contribution to the partnership. The eradication of her gender identity and her contribution to the partnership can be seen in key publications (e.g. Gilbreth, 1909, 1911, 1912) where she had considerable input as co-author, but which were credited solely to Frank (Mees, 2013; Vasquez, 2007; Lancaster, 2004; Stead, 1974). She seemed to be a willing participant in this, her own modesty preventing a more assertive approach (Mees, 2013; Graham, 1994). However, following Frank's death in 1924, Lillian was left to run both the family business, Gilbreth Inc., and the family of 12 children. Again, she faced barriers and discrimination. Work in the "man's world" (Mees, 2013) of industrial engineering and construction dried up with existing contracts cancelled and doors closed in her face by industrial and university societies when they learned of her gender (Graham, 2013). This exclusion directed her career towards training, consultancy, political advocacy and market research in areas associated with women and women's work, and ultimately to her most publicly recognised work around domestic organization and the ergonomic design of domestic workspaces.

In this chapter we move beyond motion study, for which the Gilbreths are recognised collectively, and emphasise the often overlooked contributions that Lillian brought to the partnership with Frank and then made by herself following his death. These achievements broke new ground as a woman within a context of gendered constraints so ingrained in society that on occasions Gilbreth herself demonstrated ambiguous attitudes to feminism. The chapter is organized around three areas of her work. First, we examine how her psychological perspective contributed to a humanisation of Taylorism, alongside a concern for the conditions and experience of workers which preempted the human relations movement. Second, we focus on the impact that her work had specifically on women's lives in the workplace and beyond. This included motion study work in traditionally female-dominated workplaces such as department stores; influential political advocacy on women's labour rights; and market research into sanitary napkins, which presented and influenced women's knowledge of their own bodies in ways hitherto unknown. This understanding of women as rational, intelligent consumers underpinned her later work on domesticity, which forms the final section of the chapter. While this is the work which brought Lillian Gilbreth the greatest public recognition (Mees, 2013), it is also a logical development of her humanisation of rationality, making work as easy and unobtrusive to life as possible.

Beyond rationality: the humanisation of work

The Gilbreths' motion study work is generally identified within the scientific management tradition; indeed, they were early followers of Taylor, becoming "preachers" of his "gospel of industrial efficiency" (Mees, 2013: 35). However, they diverged from Taylorist orthodoxy, instigating a "revisionist movement" (Graham, 2000: 285), which emphasised "human factors" within the workplace (Barley and Kunda, 1992: 372). They repositioned scientific management beyond rationality, focusing on more humane concerns of industrial betterment and social inclusivity. This emphasised the "motion" aspect of time and motion study, making movements easier for workers to perform and thus reducing fatigue. They condemned the stop-watch-driven "time" focus of Taylor (Mees, 2013; Lancaster, 2004), leading to a public showdown at a Taylor Society meeting in 1920 (Graham, 1997). Furthermore, the Gilbreths encountered less labour resistance than Taylorist workplaces, where Taylor struggled to gain co-operation and support from both workers and employers (Graham, 1999; Kanigel, 1997).

Gilbreth was instrumental in this humanisation, her work drawing explic-itly on psychology, a factor which made her "absolutely different" (Stead, 1974: 33) to anything else in scientific management at the time. Taylor's pur-suit of machine-like efficiency and the removal of individual skill ignored psychology and the needs and rights of individual workers (Vasquez, 2007: 55), while Gilbreth acknowledged distinct differences between workers, with the management of individuals and their feelings being key to mana-gerial success.

Gilbreth's interest in the human aspects of work arose from a semester spent at Columbia University. She studied functionalist psychology under Edward Thorndike, which emphasises learning and adaptation to situa-tions rather than taking determinist tactics, and developed a strong belief that work must be fulfilling in a way which suits each specific individual rather than the dominant Taylorist "one size fits all" approach (Graham, 1997). In her writings she emphasises the importance of individual differ-ences of workers, the importance of self-expression in work and the need for human dignity and relations (Gilbreth, 1914, 1929). Unlike Taylor's characterisation of workers as inherently lazy, Gilbreth believed workers were motivated by tasks where they were comfortable and from which they derived satisfaction, with this motivation occurring in different ways for different workers (Graham, 2000: 288). Gilbreth's humanisation of work saw efficiency as a by-product of simpler and more straightforward work, increasing productivity but not at the expense of the quality of the worker's life or of dehumanising the worker (Stead, 1974: 33; Vasquez, 2007: 59): "Efficiency in its fundamentals has to do with getting work done with the least amount of effort and the greatest amount of satisfac-tion" (Gilbreth, 1929: 61).

In articulating the value of human life and relations, Gilbreth empha-sised the importance of worker communication and co-operation and a clean working environment, with this "industrial betterment" extending to rest-rooms and the provision of reading material (Mees, 2013; Vasquez, 2007; Lancaster, 2004). The Gilbreths introduced many changes applied a decade later in the Hawthorne Studies, such as improved lighting and ventilation, rest periods and other psychological changes designed to increase worker autonomy and reduce fatigue, yet it is the likes of Mayo and Lewin who are credited as introducing these social aspects into work, with Gilbreth's contributions often overlooked (Mees, 2013; Stead, 1974):

> One could argue, in fact, that Gilbreth's emphasis on individual differences, skills, and satisfactions was an intellectual step that needed to be taken before human relations pioneers such as Mayo . . . could become cognizant of the power of the group. . . . Twentieth century management thus owes a great debt to Gilbreth's synthesis of scientific management with psychology.
>
> (Graham, 2000: 301)

Gilbreth's humanisation of scientific management foresaw other contemporary management issues and techniques, again with her name often erased from discussions of these. For example, she drew upon worker knowledge through suggestion schemes long before this was celebrated as an aspect of Japanese management (Vasquez, 2007: 56). Furthermore, her attention to reducing workplace fatigue by tailoring jobs and technology to people, rather than the other way around (Perloff and Naman, 1996), was a forerunner of ergonomics (Lancaster, 2004: 15). The emphasis was on designing tools, technology and the working environment to make the job as straightforward as possible. This helped not only with efficiency, but also in jobs where precision is important – for example, the layout of a surgical theatre is an area where the Gilbreths emphasised the simplicity of the layout (Baumgart and Neuhauser, 2009). Fitting work to the worker also inspired the Gilbreths' adaptation of work for vocational rehabilitation which allowed disabled workers, including war veterans, to participate in the labour market (Miller and Lemons, 1998:7; Gotcher, 1992). Lillian considered this to be her most important work, and continued this for decades after Frank's death, working with various presidential committees (Perloff and Naman, 1996: 110).

Building on ergonomics and fatigue reduction, the Gilbreths also saw increased productivity and worker satisfaction as being served by designing work to avoid the risk of injuries (Chaffin, 2009). In her work on nursing, Gilbreth (1935) further emphasised the importance of fatigue reduction through training, the hospital layout and the importance of not being overworked. Again, she pre-empts concerns in contemporary management. First, she recognises the emotional labour inherent in nursing (Gray, 2009), counting "emotional fatigue" (Gilbreth, 1935: 26) as one element of fatigue to be reduced within the job. Second, she outlined a forerunner of work-life balance by identifying the importance of leisure when viewing the worker holistically as a human being. Standardisation and efficiency was not about optimising output but about shortening the working day to give "opportunities for more intelligent and less fatiguing use of leisure. . . . Effective leisure presupposes serenity in the person enjoying it, and that implies economic security, physical adequacy, mental alertness, and emotional stability" (Gilbreth, 1935: 28).

Gilbreth's humanistic approach to scientific management can be viewed in the light of her and Frank's politics, which Graham (2013: 355) describes as resonating with technological progressivism of the time. She believed in the shared interests of business and citizens for progress in society, and in industrial democracy as a basis for political democracy (Graham, 2013; Stead, 1974). While this avoided the industrial unrest of Taylorism, Graham (1997: 548) suggested that it made the workers "agents of management" by aligning the interests of both parties. For Mees (2013: 35), the Gilbreths were not social radicals, but modernist social democrats who "believed in a future that was democratic, capitalistic, efficient and overwhelmingly middle class – and most of all supremely modern and useful". Such a democratic but non-radical approach is also reflected in Gilbreth's approach to women and to feminism.

Women's work and working with women

Following Frank's death, discrimination and exclusion steered Lillian's career from male-dominated industries towards areas of life traditionally associated with women. This section examines her consultancy in Macy's department stores; her application of scientific data to women's labour policy development and her market research into women as consumers. While her own achievements broke the mould of possibilities for women, she also had a direct influence on women's lives. However, she was something of a "strange candidate as a feminist", (Mees, 2013: 43) whose own career progress was achieved by "not challenging gender assumptions" (Vasquez, 2007: 49), doing little to promote women's concerns during her marriage (Nyland and Rix, 2000: 311). Her writing eschews radical approaches to feminism, demonstrating a liberal and equalities approach which demands "no favours for women", but equally "no unfair treatment" (Gilbreth, 1929: 64) This approach was informed by scientific job measurement which, following a wartime influx of women into the workplace, showed that "many more kinds of work than even the most optimistic had thought probable can be done by women". (Gilbreth, 1929: 63). This scientific method further supported her liberal approach:

> Women in industry, all women, may rejoice in an age when all facts are respectable, clear thinking and plain-speaking fashionable, and sentimentality differentiated from sentiment. . . . We no longer exalt one career over another. We no longer look up to or down on the

home-maker as different from her sisters. At least it is to be hoped that we no longer do any of these things. We have "jobs" and "workers" of both sexes in every field.

(Gilbreth, 1929: 63)

The Macy's consultancy originated with the store's head of research, Jean Lies, who examined the motion of cashier tubes while attending one of Gilbreth's courses and subsequently wished to extend scientific management throughout the store (Nyland and Rix, 2000; Graham, 2000). Eighty percent of the staff were female shop-floor workers, with the other 20% being male and predominantly in management positions. Management style was authoritarian and demeaning, with informal "counter cultures" emerging in response to this (Graham, 2000). With the shop assistants cast as "unmanageable", Gilbreth used motion study and psychology to assert control in a seemingly non-authoritarian manner (Graham, 1994: 624). Her trademark filming techniques made cashier work more productive and reduced fatigue, and she engaged in further scientific observation of the store layout and customer flow. Non-customer-facing jobs were relocated "backstage" where they were more amenable to time and motion study. Gilbreth's consultancy decreased training times while increasing control and surveillance at-a-distance over the workforce (Graham, 2000).

However, Gilbreth realised that scientific management did not transfer directly from factory to store environments. Efficiency was only one aspect of shop-floor work which added value to the store, good customer service added further value by guaranteeing repeat sales (Graham, 2000, 2013). Again, Gilbreth foresaw emotional labour, recognising that a climate of "cheerful helpfulness" (Graham, 2013: 357) improved the customer experience. In these interpersonal aspects of store work she supplemented her scientific management abilities with psychological insight. She recognised that certain personalities were better suited to interactive customer work, creating early versions of personality profiling from which workers could self-select for appropriate jobs, aided by early examples of psychometric testing (Graham, 2013). Furthermore, Gilbreth developed early instances of knowledge management and transfer (Nonaka and Takeuchi, 1995). Suggestion schemes harvested tacit knowledge about customer service from the sales staff, which was then codified in manuals as explicit knowledge, which became a property of Macy's (Graham, 2000).

Typical for Gilbreth, her work at Macy's was largely unrecognised. There was no contractual relationship (Graham, 2000: 293) – the arrangement was used, in a similar way as her uncredited writing with Frank, to further her career within existing gender constraints. However, despite Gilbreth's invisibility her work increased the visibility of women's work. From a Foucauldian disciplinary perspective, Graham (1994) suggests that job descriptions quantified the attributes for selection and that the suggestion scheme codified worker knowledge which was then used to further control and direct their actions. For Graham (1994: 631) this "realigned women's interests with those of management" and, furthermore, had anti-union leanings given that Gilbreth's psychological emphasis created happier workers who were less likely to unionise. However, a contrasting perspective views this phase of Gilbreth's career as a shift from confronting gender norms as an individual (Lancaster, 2004: 49) to a more overt confrontation of gender inequality alongside other women and women's groups (ibid.: 233). Graham (2000: 286) suggests that the co-operation between Gilbreth and Lies demonstrates the power of women's alliances in confronting the pervasive "gender mythologies" of the time:

> To manufacture a need for their expertise, Gilbreth and Lies asserted their own understanding of women's "counter cultures" and thereby played on the insecurities of managers. They may have purposefully cultivated the suspicion that they had access to the secrets of women's behavior.
>
> (Graham, 2000: 300)

In the inter-war years, Gilbreth became further involved with women's groups which addressed wages, working conditions and discrimination in the workplace (Vasquez, 2007: 58–59). This activity revolved around the Taylor Society, where both Gilbreth and Lies were part of a wider alliance of women, including Mary van Kleeck and Pauline Goldmark, taking a leading role in the second generation of scientific management (Graham, 2000: 300; Nyland and Rix, 2000: 307). They advocated scientific management as a means of solving social and industrial issues by establishing facts dispassionately rather than relying on rules of thumb (Nyland and Rix, 2000). This had a twofold impact on women. First, the recourse to facts gave a basis for argumentation counter to physical power and electoral politicking which were seen to favour male dominance. This reversed the original focus of scientific management which had privileged male "objectivity" over female "emotionalism" (Schachter, 2002: 574). Second, this style of argumentation could be applied to issues directly affecting women's social and workplace rights, such as wages and working hours (Schachter, 2002: 574), with scientific management used as an applied social science to improve the lives of women (Nyland and Rix, 2000: 312).

This work was advanced through the Industrial Relations Institute, which promoted the interests of women workers, and the US Department of Labor's Women's Bureau, where Gilbreth's scientific management was the methodology which supported the committee work of van Kleeck and Goldmark (Oldenziel, 2000). In 1926 they were Taylor Society delegates to the Department of Labour's Women's Industrial Conference, where an acrimonious split emerged. A proposal to regulate women's working hours due to health and safety concerns was met with a deregulation amendment which took a liberal/equalities approach. The amendment suggested that the legislation could lead to less female employment with employers choosing to employ men for whom working hours restrictions would not apply (Schachter, 2002; Nyland and Rix, 2000). A technical report was commissioned by the Women's Bureau, chaired by van Kleeck with Gilbreth on the three-person committee. Her scientific approach brought impartial rigour to a study which needed to be beyond reproach amid all of the recriminations and competing arguments. She used data to establish that no significant correlation occurred between women's employment patterns and changes in labour legislation. (Nyland and Rix, 2000). Gilbreth therefore played a key role in influencing women's labour market legislation:

> The sturdiness of the case made in the report muted for many years those who insisted that gender-specific labor laws necessarily reduce women's employment opportunities.
>
> (Nyland and Rix, 2000: 321)

Gilbreth's contribution to interventionist labour market legislation runs counter to her previous liberal stance on women's work. However, her participation in this activism seems to follow previous patterns, with Gilbreth very much the technical support and other people (this time van Kleeck, rather than Frank) taking the leading roles. Indeed, Lancaster (2004: 246) suggests that Gilbreth was a relatively unenthusiastic member of this group, and in later writings reverted to an equalities approach, which viewed sex divisions as "idiotic".

Further to the work on women's labour market legislation, Gilbreth also undertook activities which affected women's lives more widely. Market research into sanitary napkins, commissioned by Johnson & Johnson in 1926, saw Gilbreth engage women as consumers and uncover feminine knowledge which was hidden due to a taboo around discussing menstruation which had hindered research and development (Graham, 2013; Fouché and Vostral, 2011). Gilbreth's role was to bridge the gap between male-dominated corporations and the embodied knowledge of female consumers (Fouché and Vostral, 2011: 837). While market research was a new direction for Gilbreth, the study benefited both from her engineering knowledge in designing the napkins and her psychological knowledge in understanding the consumers (Graham, 2013: 360).

Johnson & Johnson's objective was to design and sell better sanitary products, however Gilbreth introduced further aims, including educating women as consumers, understanding how menstruation contributes to work fatigue, and refuting ideas that women were incapable of working during menstruation (Fouché and Vostral, 2011: 826; Nyland and Rix, 2000: 312). As such it fitted in with her overall goal of improving women's lives (Fouché and Vostral, 2011: 838; Lancaster, 2004: 245). The "full-blown ethnographic survey" (Fouché and Vostral, 2011: 838) of over 1,000 women's menstrual experiences provides "an invaluable source of information about women in the period between the wars". (Bullough, 1985: 617). The thoroughness of Gilbreth's approach, covering technical and psychological aspects, produced recommendations covering shape, size, design, branding, packaging, discreetness and availability of the product – all following her interest in making life straightforward, making the product "fit" with the rest of life (Bullough, 1995) and "grant[ing] women newfound agency and control of their menstrual cycles through better body mechanics" (Fouché and Vostral, 2011: 839).

For Fouché and Vostral (2011: 838), this knowledge is a translation performed by Gilbreth, making women's hitherto unspoken, tacit knowledge about their bodies intelligible as datasets to the "corporate men" at Johnson & Johnson, and ultimately commodified into intellectual property through patents. As with the tacit knowledge of shopworkers at Macy's, Gilbreth turned "situated knowledge to data" (Fouché and Vostral, 2011: 830), playing the role of "gender translator" (Fouché and Vostral, 2011: 848) or "gender mediator" (Graham, 1997: 617). Fouché and Vostral (2011: 835) note that this could be interpreted as exploitative, mining women's embodied knowledge for financial gain, with this knowledge returned to them as "purchasable items". However, they suggest an alternative interpretation (ibid.) that she "subversively" injected a feminist politics into Johnson & Johnson, enabling them to produce a feminist technology and a product based around women's wants, needs and desires which had hitherto been invisible and marginalised as "nurturing" when compared to intellectual property. In this respect, they suggest that Gilbreth "set in motion a revolution in bodily freedom and mobility for women, a revolution that was largely immeasurable and invisible to a masculine system of progress" (Fouché and Vostral, 2011: 846). Gilbreth further recommended that women be involved in all future product development, this was reflected in the advertising slogan: "Women designed Modess" (Graham, 2013: 361). However, despite this female visibility, Gilbreth's own contribution was again rendered invisible: she was not credited for her work and not recognised within the patents, nor was she salaried (Fouché and Vostral, 2011: 847).

Defined by domesticity

Gilbreth undertook further market research on other products for women (Bullough, 1985: 617) before turning to domesticity and homemaking. While this latter part of her career most often defines Gilbreth in the public eye, especially thanks to *Cheaper by the Dozen*, it also reflects how gendered constraints and expectations shaped her entire career trajectory. Her focus on domesticity arose not from a genuine interest but as a realignment of her career following Frank's death and from being objectified by mass media as mother to 12 children (Graham, 1994). She needed to develop her own distinct reputation, but at the same time the domestic engineering arena was growing and providing intense competition. In her favour were her engineering work experience, a doctorate in psychology and her fame as a mother – a combination which "made her more intriguing to the public" (Graham, 1999: 651). She argued that women could be "intelligent consumers" in kitchen and appliance design, realising that she could "have it all ways" (Lancaster, 2004: 248) if she presented herself as an expert in women's work and household management.

This section examines Gilbreth's work on domesticity, noting how it reflects both her humanisation of Taylorism and the "ambiguous gender politics" (Lancaster, 2004: 256) found earlier in her career. In this latter respect, she invites critique for reinforcing domestic gender divisions: "[a]n unfortunate part of Gilbreth's legacy is that many women today continue to feel the sole responsibility for maximising efficiency and psychological health within their homes" (Graham, 1999: 667). Alongside this are a number of wry comments that focus on her own inability to cook or which deride her for hiring domestic help, such as a live-in handyman and a housekeeper, while also allocating chores to her children and drawing on family members to help out (Levey, 2001). Here we have an apparent paradox in that her children hindered her career but that outsiders were used to make sure they didn't – a contradiction which goes against simple reductionist critique (Graham, 1994: 627) Indeed, Gilbreth's focus on domesticity can be viewed as reframing housework, defeminising the work and making it a group responsibility (Lancaster, 2004) while at the same time recasting women as intelligent, rational consumers.

In this respect, Gilbreth's work in integrating new technologies into the kitchen (Graham, 2013) bought her workplace concerns with fatigue reduction to women, who predominantly bore the burden of homemaking. She aimed to "ease the drudgery of housework, not to redistribute it" (Graham, 1999: 645). Again, Gilbreth took a humane approach to efficiency which recognised individual differences and which encouraged women to enjoy life away from the household and family, similar to the argument she made about the work-life balance of nurses. She further argued that housework was in fact work and should be delegated and made a group responsibility rather than the sole responsibility of the homemaker (Gilbreth, 1927). This view was shared with contemporary radical feminists (Lancaster, 2004), and Gilbreth was vocal about the need for men and children to contribute equally to homemaking (Gilbreth, 1927) as a means of bringing happiness in life by creating time to spend on more enjoyable activities (Lancaster, 2004). Gilbreth argued that women should take responsibility for their own psychological well-being, avoiding being unselfish and sacrificing their own time and personal interests for the sake of the household.

Her approach to domestic design contrasts with the contemporaneous work of the architect Le Corbusier, who applied Taylorist ideas to domestic design. Unlike Gilbreth, Le Corbusier focused solely on efficiency and ignored individuality and comfort, emphasising a "one best way" approach: "human needs were universal and could be uniformalized, and consequently his solutions were prototypical, not personal" (Rybczynski, 1987: 191). Gilbreth criticised the impracticality of "male-designed" kitchens (Lancaster, 2004: 255), arguing that domestic design is not a blueprint and people should adapt for their own needs (ibid.: 265), as she did by adjusting worktops to suit her height (Land, 2005). This follows Gilbreth's first two rules for domestic efficiency – "Be guided by convenience, not convention" and "Consider the personalities and habits of your family, yourself included" (Gilbreth, Thomas and Clymer, 1954: 158, cited by Rybcznski, 1987: 191). Gilbreth used scientific management techniques such as flow charts and micro-motion transfer sheets but was much more concerned with convenience, colour and choice, providing an applied form of Taylorism which focused on meeting the end users' needs and providing comfortable domestic surroundings. Her work thus has a human quality which was lacking in the prescriptive "efficiency over comfort" ethos adopted by Le Corbusier and others in the modernist architectural movement. However, while her ideas have been the most enduring, with the kitchen "triangle" still featuring in contemporary domestic design, Le Corbusier is arguably the more renowned. Once again Gilbreth's work is marginalised in the shadow of others.

While easing and defeminising domestic work, Gilbreth extended her view, developed in the market research on sanitary products, that women were rational, intelligent consumers (Fouché and Vostral, 2011: 842) where "[the] roles of 'efficient homemaker', 'responsible mother', and 'intelligent consumer' were woven together" (Graham, 1997: 49). This view of women ran counter to prevailing norms, reflected in advertising, which "pulled on women's heartstrings, emotions and instinctual drives" (Graham, 2013: 366). With over 85% of household spending done by women (Graham,

2013: 359), Gilbreth combined her scientific and psychological background with her role as gender mediator and her belief that products should be designed and tailored for the people using them (Graham, 1997).

The work on domesticity is a microcosm of Gilbreth's multifaceted life and work, from early expectations to forego a professional career for a domestic, homemaking role to the marginalised position of women in society steering her professional career towards domestic concerns. While this focus invited criticism for reinforcing such marginalisation, it is from within this position that Gilbreth aimed to improve the lives of women by using her engineering and psychological knowledge to reduce the fatigue of domestic work, to redistribute the responsibility for such work and to give women agency as rational consumers, while breaking through new ground herself as a woman. As suggested by Gibson et al. (2015), she was successful both despite being, and because she was, a woman.

Conclusion

There are many contradictions and complexities in Gilbreth's "multi-dimensional" (Graham, 2013: 365) life and legacy. As a "multiple, protean, fluid, fragmented and heterogeneous" individual (Graham, 1994: 639), she possessed many different subject selves as Frank's assistant and servant to the needs of their children, forced out of industrial management by sex discrimination, but at the same time portrayed as "superwoman" (Graham, 1994: 626; Gibson et al., 2015; Vasquez, 2007). She was a polymath (Vasquez, 2007: 46) who covered many roles including engineer, psychologist, academic, consultant, author, policy-maker, homemaker and pioneer, any one of which would be worthy of a career in itself.

This complex feminine identity left people unable to categorise Gilbreth, who was celebrated in the media for both her career and family (Lancaster, 2004: 331). Her impact upon women is also ambiguous: she both reinforced and contradicted traditional gender roles (Lancaster, 2004: 6). She was very much a woman of her time and did not challenge gendered assumptions about the role of women. Rather than eradicating the gendered constraints and obstacles that she faced, she found ways around them, taking different paths (Vasquez, 2007: 46). At the same time, she achieved much which improved the lives of workers generally and of women in particular. She took positions that improved the quality of women's work, advocated a reduction of the domestic division of labour, improved women's labour market rights and gave agency to women as rational consumers, and in doing so also articulated women's embodied knowledge of their own bodies. She strongly believed that women's voices should be heard and that women had to take responsibility for this themselves, not acting as passive bystanders. While her work "changed the space of possibilities of person-hood for women" (Graham, 1994: 635), her pioneering achievements broke considerable new ground as a woman. In this respect, Lancaster (2004: 1) suggests that Gilbreth was an "agent and representative" of the important social change at the time of women moving into the workplace.

And yet much of her pioneering work has been largely overlooked by organizational writers and management theorists alike. Her work has informed many areas of organizational and domestic life, with its focus on the alleviation of fatigue and a psychologically informed humanisation of scientific management, which was the forerunner of many areas of man-agement theory and practice that exist today. One only has to delve into current areas of interest such as work-life balance, ergonomics and knowl-edge management to see how her initial ideas have held their currency and value, and we suggest that her work remains relevant for students of contemporary management and organization studies. While her work did much for women, her wider contributions to management theory and practice are often rendered invisible compared to her husband, her male contemporaries and many of the male theorists whose work she foresaw. We present the chapter to both recognise and celebrate the work of Lillian Moller Gilbreth and to provide visibility to her work that might redress this imbalance.

Notes

1 "Gilbreth" refers solely to Lillian Gilbreth. Where both Gilbreths are being dis-cussed, they will be referred to as "Lillian" and "Frank".
2 Many other articles and biographies list Gilbreth's achievements in detail (e.g. Vasquez (2007); Graham (1998)).

Recommended reading

Original text by Gilbreth

Gilbreth, Lillian M. 1914. *The Psychology of Management: The Function of the Mind in Determining, Teaching and Installing Methods of Least Waste.* New York, NY: Sturgis & Walton (Lillian's original and unrewarded Ph.D. thesis).

Key academic text

http://earchives.lib.purdue.edu/cdm/search/searchterm/lillian%20gilbreth/(Purdue University's archives have video, photographic and documentary artefacts relat-ing to Lillian Gilbreth).

Accessible resource

Lancaster, Jane. 2004. *Making Time: Lillian Moller Gilbreth: A Life beyond Cheaper by the Dozen.* Lebanon, NH: University Press of New England.

References

Barley, S. R., and G. Kunda. 1992. "Design and devotion: Surges of rational and normative ideologies of control in managerial discourse." *Administrative Science Quarterly* 37: 363–399.

Baumgart, A., and D. Neuhauser. 2009. "Frank and Lillian Gilbreth: Scientific management in the operating room." *Quality & Safety in Health Care* 18 (5): 413–415.

Bullough, V. L. 1985. "Merchandising the sanitary napkin: Lillian Gilbreth's 1927 survey." *Signs: Journal of Women in Culture and Society* 10 (3): 615–627.

Chaffin, D. B. 2009. "The evolving role of biomechanics in prevention of overexertion injuries." *Ergonomics* 52 (1): 3–14.

Fouché, R., and S. Vostral. 2011. "Selling women: Lillian Gilbreth, gender translation, and intellectual property." *American University Journal of Gender, Social Policy & the Law.* 19: 825.

Gibson, J. W., R. W. Clayton, J. Deem, J. E. Einstein, and E. L. Henry. 2015. "Viewing the work of Lillian M. Gilbreth through the lens of critical biography." *Journal of Management History* 21 (3): 288–308.

Gilbreth, F. B. 1909. *Bricklaying System.* New York, NY: M. C. Clark.

Gilbreth, F. B. 1911. *Motion Study: A Method for Increasing the Efficiency of the Workman.* New York, NY: David Van Norstrand.

Gilbreth, F. B. 1912. *Primer of Scientific Management.* New York, NY: David Van Norstrand.

Gilbreth, F. B., and E. G. Carey. 1949. *Cheaper by the dozen.* London: William Heinemann.

Gilbreth, L. M. 1914. *The Psychology of Management: The Function of the Mind in Determining, Teaching and Installing Methods of Least Waste.* New York, NY: Sturgis & Walton.

Gilbreth, L. M. 1927. *The Homemaker and Her Job.* New York, NY: Appleton.

Gilbreth, L. M. 1929. "Efficiency of women workers." *Annals of the American Academy of Political and Social Science* 143 (1): 61–64.

Gilbreth, L. M. 1935. "Fatigue as it affects nursing." *American Journal of Nursing* 35 (1): 25–28.

Gilbreth, L. M., Thomas, O. M., and Clymer, E. 1954. *Management in the Home.* New York, NY: Dood, Mead & Co.

Gotcher, J. M. 1992. "Assisting the handicapped: The pioneering efforts of Frank and Lillian Gilbreth." *Journal of Management* 18 (1): 5–13.

Graham, L. D. 1994. "Critical biography without subjects and objects: An encounter with Dr. Lillian Moller Gilbreth." *Sociological Quarterly* 35 (4): 621–643.

Graham, L. D. 1997. "Beyond manipulation: Lillian Gilbreth's industrial psychology and the governmentality of women consumers." *Sociological Quarterly* 38 (4): 539–565.

Graham, L. D. 1998. *Managing on Her Own: Dr. Lillian Gilbreth and Women's Work in the Interwar Era*. Norcross, GA: Engineering & Management Press.

Graham, L. D. 1999. "Domesticating efficiency: Lillian Gilbreth's scientific management of homemakers, 1924–1930." *Signs: Journal of Women in Culture and Society* 24 (3): 633–675.

Graham, L. D. 2000. "Lillian Gilbreth and the mental revolution at Macy's, 1925–1928." *Journal of Management History (Archive)* 6 (7): 285–305.

Graham, L. D. 2013. "Lillian Gilbreth's psychologically enriched scientific management of women consumers." *Journal of History Research in Marketing* 5 (3): 351–369.

Gray, B. 2009. "The emotional labour of nursing: Defining and managing emotions in nursing work." *Nurse Education Today* 29 (2): 168–175.

Heames, J., J. T. Heames, and J. W. Breland. 2010. "Management pioneer contributors: 30-year review." *Journal of Management History* 16 (4): 427–436.

Kanigel, R. 1997. *The One Best Way: Frederick Winslow Taylor and the Enigma of Efficiency*. New York, NY: Viking.

Lancaster, J. 2004. *Making Time: Lillian Moller Gilbreth: A Life beyond Cheaper by the Dozen*. Lebanon, NH: University Press of New England.

Land, L. 2005. "Counterintuitive: How the marketing of modernism hijacked the kitchen stove." In *From Betty Crocker to Feminist Food Studies: Critical Perspectives on Women and Food*, edited by A. V. Avakian and B. Haber, 41–61. Liverpool: Liverpool University Press.

Levey, J. F. 2001. "Imagining the family in US post-war popular culture: The case of the Egg and I and Cheaper by the Dozen." *Journal of Women's History* 13 (3): 125–150.

Mees, B. 2013. "Mind, method, and motion: Frank and Lillian Gilbreth." In *The Oxford Handbook of Management Theorists*, edited by M. Witzel and M. Warner, 32–48. Oxford: Oxford University Press.

Miller, T. R., and M. A. Lemons. 1998. "Breaking the glass ceiling: Lessons from a management pioneer." *SAM Advanced Management Journal* 63 (1): 4.

Nonaka, I., and H. Takeuchi. 1995. *The Knowledge-Creating Company: How Japanese Companies Create the Dynamics of Innovation*. Oxford: Oxford University Press.

Nyland, C., and M. Rix. 2000. "Mary van Kleeck, Lillian Gilbreth and the Women's Bureau study of gendered labor law." *Journal of Management History (Archive)* 6 (7): 306–322.

Oldenziel, R. 2000. "Gender and scientific management: Women and the history of the International Institute for Industrial Relations, 1922–1946." *Journal of Management History* 6 (7): 323–342.

Perloff, R, and J. L. Naman. 1996. "Lillian Gilbreth: Tireless advocate for a general psychology." In *Portraits of Pioneers in Psychology*, edited by G. A. Kimble, C. A. Boneau, and M. Wertheimer, 107–118, vol. 2. Mahwah, NJ: Lawrence Erlbaum Associates.

Rybczynski, W. 1987. *Home: A Short History of an Idea*. New York, NY: Penguin.

Schachter, H. L. 2002. "Women, progressive-era reform, and scientific management." *Administration & Society* 34 (5): 563–578.

Stead, B. A. 1974. "Women's contributions to management thought." *Business Horizons* 17 (1): 32–36.

Vasquez, M.J.T. 2007. "Lillian Evelyn Moller Gilbreth: The woman who had it all." In *Women of Vision: Their Psychology, Circumstances, and Success*, edited by A. J. Clamar, E. A. Gavin, and M. A. Siderits, 45–60. Springer series, focus on women. New York, NY: Springer.

Wren, D. A. 1972. "In Memoriam: Lillian Moller Gilbreth (1878–1972)." *Academy of Management Journal* 15 (1): 7–8.

Wren, D. A., and R. D. Hay. 1977. "Management historians and business historians: Differing perceptions of pioneer contributors." *Academy of Management Journal* 20 (3): 470–476.

5 The inspirations of Heather Höpfl

Taking heart from radical humanism

Achilleas Karayiannis and Monika Kostera

Organising myself
by Heather Höpfl

Organising Myself.

Well, the thing about getting myself organised is that
I need to keep classifying and making lists and
Crossing things off and putting things on and
Making fresh lists and finding myself with a never ending
list, of lists, of lists, of tasks, and tasks, and endless
Classifications.

Well, the thing about getting myself organised is that
I need to keep making piles of things of different sorts
A pile of administration, a pile of papers to review,
A pile of things to do, which is endless and which always
Moves, topples, collapses as more piles are created
Which cover the dining room table, cover the living room
floor, cover the bedroom floor, until I am surrounded
By things to do and piles of work, which are endless.

Well, the thing about getting myself organised is that
I have to make sure I have a clean supply of underwear and
Blouses, and socks. I find that I must keep feeding the
washing machine and must keep myself reasonably clean. There
is so little time or space for getting myself organised
between the clean piles of washing, work in progress and
endless lists. Everything reduces to taxonomy.

Well, the thing is . . . I will never be organised until the
day I retire – and that, God willing. It is now too difficult
to pull back from the mountains of lists and piles of work and
clean underwear. My garden is overgrown and hardly a surface
in my house is free. I think I must become more disorganised
and defy classification, throw away my lists, kick over the
piles of work and think about being.

Well, the thing about being myself is . . . great!
And so I conclude that there are broadly two forms of
organisation:
One – the tyrannical taxonomies which destroy the spirit
Two – ordering which creates space, music, harmonies.

Let our projects be subversions and liberation.

Let's create the spaces which defy classification and resist
subjection. I send you peace. Let's go forward in the power
of other ways of knowing. And. I will stop trying to organise
myself for classification and consumption – I will try to
organise myself to be. Ah Life. To smell the warm sweet
smells of a Summer evening, to breathe fresh air, to live at
ease with the world, to enjoy my children, to be.

13th of July 1995

Personal stories

Heather Höpfl used to say that the social, the organizational, the political
is always personal. To her, a social science that does not resonate with the
personal is meaningless. This is precisely why she preferred ethnographic
and qualitative research: it focuses on people and sheds light on the human
side of the organization. Therefore, we decided to include a particularly
extensive personal note on Heather, our recollection of meeting her and
working with her. Not just the contents of her work, but the way she engaged
in it, carries a significance as part of her legacy: the way she was as a human
being, colleague and scholar. She was an author who lived the way she
was teaching. In this text, we would like to commemorate and invoke her
presence the way she herself believed in: as a personalised social science
narrative.

Image 5.1 Heather Höpfl at the Arts of Management conference, Kraków, 2006

Monika

I met Heather at a rather unusual conference back in 1994. There were several people who were upset and even distressed, and Heather was comforting them. She spoke in long, complicated sentences, with a cascading rhythm, and that fascinated me. I have been spellbound by words and sentences since I was a small child, and I am sure if someone liked to hypnotise me by talking that way, they easily could. I remember thinking, *I wish she'd speak to me*. But she was too busy and I was too introverted. Seeking peace and quiet to read, I found a nice, completely empty little chapel on the conference premises. There was warm light streaming in through the stained glass windows and cool shadows flowing through the middle of the floor. And then, suddenly, she came in and sat down in the same chapel, smiling. I put aside my book. We sat there both in silence and it was completely good. When we left the little oratory, walking side by side, I felt as if we have been friends for a long time. Many years later, she said she'd felt the same way. I was not at all surprised when she invited me to the UK for a conference she was organizing the next year. She was not surprised when I turned up with a little icon of an unusually cheerful and rosy cheeked Virgin Mary for her, which I suspected she would enjoy.

Bolton 1995. It was a good conference: it felt like a dream, with so many of my favourite authors attending – people I've known as names in the texts I loved to read. The mood was unlike all other conferences I had attended so far: friendly and informal, with everyone acting as if they had known each other for ages – which they probably did. But they acted like that towards me too, which was much more than I had dared to expect. Heather was at the centre of a huge centrifuge of brilliance; she had this influence on moods and people. Things happened around her. The world was not flat then, not yet; academia was rock 'n' roll, words mattered, nobody sane thought of money at universities. People smoked – a lot. I did too, as did Heather. I have an image of her from that conference, standing in a pool of April sunshine, with a cigarette in her hand, telling me about the North of England of her childhood and of more recent years. Her hands were moving, gentle and expressive in the honey-coloured light. Many years later, in what turned out to be one of our last communications, she said:

> This is the north. So different from the south . . . I love the north east – we are about one and a half hours north of Sheffield. These great 19C northern towns have a Victorian legacy, grand architecture with dark Gothic undertones. Large civic buildings and grand parks. Lovely people: honest and frank in their views. To be honest I never liked the south much . . . . . .[1]

After that conference there were many others. She visited Warsaw. I visited her in the North. Wherever we met, we tended to spend much time together: smoking, talking, or sitting in silence; images fusing with one another, linking together the spaces and moments in time.

Once, when she was visiting me in Warsaw, the snow suddenly started to fall thick and white, and the darkness between was soft, like an old-fashioned cushion. We met in the city centre and intended to go to see an art exhibition, but all public transport stood virtually still. So instead, we walked a long way in the falling snow to a restaurant in the park that we both liked. She told me how she, the previous night, was standing in the hotel window watching trams, and how it looked just like an electric storm when the pantographs sparked. A third vivid image of her stayed with me: her presence against the cold yet strangely kind winter background and the sparking trams.

I was doing fieldwork in one of my alternative organizations, a vegan restaurant in Warsaw, when I learned about her death. I stood up and went out from the kitchen where I was sitting and taking notes. The room was full of people, and suddenly felt huge. There was a stream of light pouring in through the middle and balls of shadows unfurling in the corners. The chubby waitress

Image 5.2 Monika Kostera and Heather Höpfl in Turku, Finland, at SCOS 1995

was chatting with a suited man stooped by the bar; she was smiling warmly at him as he was telling her about the woes of his workplace, presumably one of the nearby banks. There was a woman with dreadlocks sitting by the back wall, breastfeeding a small child. I thought: *images of Madonna – you would have liked it, dear Heather, you like images of the Madonna.*

So this one is for you, Friend and Colleague: images of what cannot be put into form, which spill over and unfurl from where most of us do not know how to look.

Achilleas

The first meeting: 18 October 2005

I dedicated the entire month of September 2005 looking at the profiles and research interests of the academic staff at the then AFM (Accounting, Finance, Management) department of the University of Essex. I was fascinated by Heather's work on dramaturgy and aesthetics, especially the article "Playing the Part: Reflections on Aspects of Mere Performance in the Customer-Client Relationship" (2002b) and the book she had co-written with Stephen Linstead, *The Aesthetics of Organization* (2000). I had also looked into the work of C. W., who eventually became my second supervisor, and I. K., who chaired most of the meetings with regard to the progression of my doctoral research.

I met Heather for the first time on 18 October 2005; in an email I sent to her on 17 October 2005, Heather's reply was:

> Yes . . . . [it was very typical for Heather to use dots in her emails!] see you at 11 a.m. H.

One of Heather's very first questions to me was to name three types of food that I like to eat. I told her that these were chicken, avocado and pasta. My then PhD colleagues S. M., P. P. and S. M. will clearly remember these, since in the occasions that I was cooking for them the menu was likely to include them. Eventually I got to understand that in Heather's supervision, the establishment of relationships between different elements, ideas and thoughts was very important: the heart and the soul, the body and the mind. Heather advised me to bring my origins, Cyprus and Greece, into my research, hence the fact that after a few months, I chose Cyprus Airways and the Theatrical Organization of Cyprus as the two case studies of my doctoral research. Furthermore, Heather asked me to read a book that reflects my origins. I suggested *Zorba the Greek* (2000), and in order to introduce me to the dramaturgical work of other people, Heather suggested Erving Goffman's *The Presentation of Self in Everyday Life* (1959). Wow, no textbooks involved!

And then . . . (2005–2012)

The last time I saw Heather was on 19 October 2012, seven years and a day after our first meeting. Heather visited Cyprus with her husband Harro Höpfl, in order to attend my wedding. I had started writing the final draft version of this part of the book chapter on 17 October 2017. If anything, after realising these coincidences, I feel even more that Heather is actually here. With me. In between and rising above the lines.

During these seven years, every time I was seeing the sceptical part of Heather's character, she would lower her glasses, raise her eyebrows and look over her glasses directly into the eyes of the person she would be addressing. She would either engage in a prolonged version of what she was to say, or simply acknowledge her company's words by saying "yes . . . yes" while nodding with her head, showing that she was following what her company was saying. I can already see my co-students, her supervisees, colleagues and friends smiling.

The viva examination: 10–11 May 2009

My colleague P. P. (Heather's supervisee, too) and I had our VIVA examination on 11 May 2009. P. P. ended up taking the morning session. In retrospect, I feel that this worked well for both of us. He passed with minor changes, laying the anxiety off his shoulders earlier and I was motivated by his success; it was one of the two incidents that pushed me forward. The second was an invitation by Heather to both P. and myself to her home for brunch on the day before the VIVA examination. When we sat around the table, Harro advised us that when we are asked a question, we should wait for a few seconds, giving the impression that we are indeed thinking about the question, even if were so impatient to answer. Fascinating. I assume that my examiners would have no problem with me appearing to think – as long as the job was done, successfully.

On 10 May, Heather was simultaneously present and absent. I don't remember a single word from her. I don't remember any piece of advice. But she was there, physically and in spirit. She had faith that we would both make her proud on the very following day. And we did. On 10 and 11 May, it was probably the very first time that I realised how much Heather believed in me. Exactly one month after the VIVA, I received the last email from her, regarding three minor changes that still needed attention, using, again, dots as a defining characteristic of her writing style:

> The rest is fine . . . . have the corrections done over the weekend – 10 min job.

The journey was over! It began on 3 October 2005 and ended officially with my graduation on 17 July 2009 – a journey during which Heather proved to be more than an academic "Mother". She was my mentor, my friend, one of the most important persons in my life and definitely the one that has shaped my academic writing and research interests more than anyone else. Descartes said "I think therefore I am"; and Heather taught me how to think fully and thus fully to become. Thank you.

An overview of Heather's body of work: some key texts

Heather Höpfl[2] brought humanist and emancipatory perspectives into organization studies, including ethnographic, aesthetic, dramaturgical and feminist ideas. Her most well-known writings are on otherness/othering. Her

Image 5.3 Heather Höpfl in Lancaster, 1997

interest in organizational motherhood, and herself being one of the founding mothers of humanistic management, make her a strong female presence in organization theory. Due to her untimely death, Heather was unable to draw her body of work together into a single whole; her intellectual fertility and imaginativeness in any case meant that she was always discovering new avenues to explore. Heather was and continues to be a strong and graceful influence in organization studies, especially for scholars interested in the humanistic dimension of organizing.[3]

Heather believed social science should be written as Walter Benjamin was doing it – such that each era, no matter what the current trends, rules and fashions are, leaves only the Benjamins to its successors. Heather did not approve of the formalised, impersonal and often formulaic academic writing typical of recent decades, and she certainly would not have wanted to have a text dedicated to her written in this manner. What follows is an attempt to do it the way she would have liked it. Although we do not claim anything like Benjamin's or Höpfl's talent, we nonetheless share with both one important feature in our writing style, one that Heather took very seriously: the personal.

Humanistic management

Heather Höpfl was one of the three founding mothers of humanistic management, the two others being Mary Parker Follett and Simone Weil (Kostera, 2016). Her writings are poetic, multilayered and quite multifaceted. Heather had a style of writing that kept shining through in her books and conference papers as well as her research articles. Her presentations were always strikingly dramatic – she liked throwing several ideas up into the air and ended up gracefully catching them. Heather used to speak in a musical voice, tending toward unpretentious melorecitation, taking up themes that were profoundly human: feelings, relationships, spirituality, hopes and how they related to organizational settings. Heather was particularly interested in the roles humans play in organizations and their broader cultural, political and institutional context. Heather never shunned complexity and she staunchly refused to adopt reductionism, even for the sake of argument or, even less, in order to get published. In her own words:

> I have tried to respect the reviewers' suggestions that I make the text and the language more accessible. There is a considerable dilemma in this. Of course, they are entirely right in asking what conclusions should be drawn. I have tried to make the ideas more transparent. At the same time, I am already ensnared more than I would wish in the trajectory of the text, I am conscious of regulation in my working life through a whole series of matrix structures. I am enslaved to the logic of organizing and to practices which I observe to do harm. The absurd rhetoric of change management is pervasive. And, this? Well, perhaps it is just romantic. Then again, perhaps it is just about finding the Mother.
> (Höpfl, 2000d, p. 32)

Among the multiple and intricately interconnected issues, Heather addressed were the following: how people and organizations learn and develop; how the managers and the managed differ and how they are basically the same, depending on each other but rarely acknowledging the mutuality of the relationship; how reflection and sincerity can set us free. Heather regarded organizational power as a force that is often violent yet superficial, reliant on a rhetoric that promises control but, in reality, offers no more than an obsessive avoidance of ambivalence and silence. As a counterweight

Heather proposed poetics, running below the surface, a source of alternative power making it possible for the underdog to offer a resistance that springs the heart, from the core of what it means to be human. Poetics was, to her, a repository of counter-power for liberation and emancipation. This is also the role of theatre, which Heather understood as a sacred ritual unfolding on different levels of social reality from the superficial to the dark and invisible unconscious that connects us all. To comprehend it meant, to her, being equipped with a potential to survive in a world increasingly defined by management based on violence, fear and suppression of the personal.

Heather liked to emphasise the role of silence as a mode of learning, making it possible to see what is institutionally hidden from sight and to understand complexity. Like actors about to enter the stage, social actors need to be able to draw a deep breath in silence so that they can resist dehumanisation and realise that their roles have a poetic underpinning, which can help them to play their roles differently. In the end, poetics will prevail because it runs deeper than the rhetoric. When the masque falls, actors equipped with poetic consciousness are able to transcend the imperative of superficial reductionist control and invoke managerial roles rooted in organizational motherhood.

In this text we will focus on the two aspects of Heather Höpfl's work that we regard as central in the legacy she has left us with: theatre and poetics. We will not strive for a comprehensive or detailed presentation or exegesis of her writings; we only propose a broad sketch of ideas that we consider principal in her scholarship.

Work on theatre and organization

Heather Höplf's interest in theatre was both empirical and epistemological. As Ilaria Boncori points out, Heather tended to investigate relationships and meanings "stemming from the image in connection with other scenes, actors, statements, signifiers and symbols" (Boncori, 2017: 101), and so theatre is most obviously present in Heather's work as an interpretive framework. For example, in the text "Playing the Part: Reflections on Aspects of Mere Performance in the Customer-Client Relationship" (2002b), Heather reflects some of her work with British Airways in the 1990s, especially with regard to the company's safety culture and brand image. Heather describes in detail her experience as a passenger in one of the British Airways flights from London to Kraków in 1999, where the cabin crew members produced an out of role/character performance in order to make the flight a memorable experience for the passengers. Heather comments: "I can play this role because I am detached from it" (Höpfl, 2002b, p. 260), in order to suggest that the cabin crew members were so good in producing the play simply because they were able to disassociate themselves as personas from the characters they were representing, but they were not, in real life. Bertolt Brecht (1964) best reflects this through his Epic Theatre and the notion of alienation, which argues that the best performances come when there is a clear dividing line between the person and the character.

In other words, the memorable experience on this British Airways flight was created exactly because the passengers saw an unexpected performance that was not in line with the usual play performed in front of their eyes in any flight they experienced before in their life. Moreover, the memorable experience was created because the cabin crew members managed to make the passengers feel that the cabin crew members as personas were not the characters they were performing. Heather Höpfl, Chris Steyaert, Stefan Meisiek, Daniel Hjorth, Hans Hansen and Dorthe Bille (2006), argue that theatre itself is the space where the most dramatic transitions and transformations take place, and it is exactly this reasoning that can serve to explain the "logic" behind the out-of-character and out-of-role performances presented by the cabin crew members of the British Airways flight. The authors believe that on the theatrical stage, dramatic transitions and transformations take place when the actors consciously assume roles that might be in complete antithesis to the roles they consciously or unconsciously assume in their personal and social lives.

Yet the theatrical dimension of social life can be transformative all by itself, as a way of organizing and as a way of thinking. Georg Schreyögg and Heather Höpfl (2004) note that a central principle of the dramaturgical approach to the study of social phenomena is the use of "the metaphor of social life as theatre" (p. 691), placing emphasis not only on the actions of individuals but also in the analysis that the individuals, as the actors of such actions, give to them. If an organization is a microcosm that reflects the society within which it is situated, then it suffices to argue that the metaphor of social life can be used to reflect life within this microcosm too. Moreover, Schreyögg and Höpfl argue that

> one theoretical interest in the use of theatre as a metaphor is in the points at which sustaining the illusion, continuing to play out the drama, becomes too great for the actor to bear; this alienation of the actor from the performance.
>
> (Schreyögg and Höpfl, 2004: p. 692)

This, potentially, provides justification for the exaggerated, out-of-character performance on behalf of the cabin crew members in the British Airways flight from London to Kraków. By detaching, alienating themselves as personas from their character and role (Brecht, 1964) as cabin crew members, the cabin crew members managed to perform a play that served as a memorable experience for the passengers. Referring to Pine and Gilmore's *The Experience Economy* (1999), Daniel Hjorth and Monika Kostera (2007) believe that "the producers of dramatic and individualized offerings seem to stand above those experiencing, as if the suppliers' minds resided over the bodies of their customers" (Hjorth and Kostera, 2007: 11). The dramatic impulse produces the fabric of social interaction, including social roles.

But it goes much deeper than defining institutions and interactions. The dramatic creates an expression for such fundamental components of social life as identity and alterity. The aspect of identity is depicted in the text "The Aesthetics of Reticence" (2000), where Heather Höpfl gives a very descriptive and personal account of the feelings that she went through when the school that she left in 1967 was not there when she returned for a visit to Runcorn, her hometown, in the north-west of England. The absence, rather than the presence, of the school created within Heather a sense of deprivation, in that there were so many feelings and emotions that she needed to address, but she couldn't due to the absence of the school. There was an inability to assign her experiences with the school that she had been to for a few years and consequently felt a discomfort in having to keep these experiences within her. Heather frames this lack in a vivid dramatic imagery: her emotions were homeless, in that

> the space into which they could have been projected was now occupied (by the school not being where it used to be, by the school not being anywhere) and, moreover, occupied in such a way as to prevent any engagement with the history of the site.
>
> (Linstead and Höpfl, 2000, p. 94)

Heather was overwhelmed by that absence, like a character invoked by an absence on the stage. The absence of the school reduced her own history into experiences that could no longer be related to a physical location and reality, thus creating a turning point in the unfolding drama of life.

The meaning of alterity is also defined dramatically. Barbara Czarniawska and Heather Höpfl (2002) argue that the production of the Other is problematic on many levels, from personal, via organizational, to societal. Stanislavski's method actor presents a version of reality, as this is brought forward by the specific actor who acts on the specific role and character and uses it to show that this version of reality is actually the only version of reality. Casting a shadow therefore is not so much a choice but much more a contested effort on behalf of the individual to mimic and perhaps caricature the original through the production of his or her own replicas (Czarniawska and Höpfl, 2002). Everyday life in organizations sees the Other as a concern through diversity management but in the process of it, differences become subsumed within the prevailing, authentic, more objective understanding of the one reality that is taking place. There are therefore implications when constructing a more theatrical persona and assessing its performance on the basis of how much individual and organizational behaviour is regulated through manipulation of the role (Höpfl, 1995a).

Finally, as we have already suggested, there is a thread throughout Heather's theatrical work on organizing and organization referring to emptiness as a most powerful stage presence. The idea of the empty space was introduced by Peter Brook in his book *The Empty Space* (1968), who suggested that Stanislavski wanted his actors to embody their characters on stage so that the audience was to be watching the real reality of life:

> the Method Actor was trained to reject cliché imitations of reality and to search for something more real in himself. He then had to represent this through the living of it, and so acting became a deeply naturalistic study.
>
> (Brook, 1968: 30)

Just as Heather was experiencing the absence of the school in her very own particular way, the actor would be using the space given to him or her on stage in order to embody the character in his or her own way and present the character so realistically, as if this was the one objective and authentic version of the character and the role. The empty space can be seen as an active possibility, an invocation of our creativity and perhaps a creativity that is greater than ourselves: "that sphere of reality which is unclassified and unclaimed, the margin where change can be initiated" (Kostera, 2000, p: 2).

To Heather, the dramaturgical potential was, ultimately, about that: the offering of a connection beyond the superficial, linear and predetermined. The potential is fundamental and can liberate and transform. By developing a theatrical sensibility, social actors can embrace the potentiality of the stage to free imagination and empathy and thus work to transcend the seemingly irresistible restraints of everyday on-stage performances which

> in order to manifest [create] a supreme deceit: to manufacture a compelling illusion. The employee who prepares for the assumption of the organizational role is comparable to the preparation of the actor for the assumption of the dramatic mask. The major difference is the apparent degree of discretion on improvisation which is permitted around the role.
>
> (Höpfl, 2002a)

Work on organizational poetics

Heather's profound interest for emptiness informed her other major area of inspiration and conception, citing the Aristotelean distinction between poetics and rhetorics (Höpfl, 1995b). While the former is based on ambiguity, the latter aims at explicitness, order and a clear narrative thrust. Poetics creates resonances for what is not fully defined, sometimes impossible to express. It does so with the help of words, as well as with silences and empty spaces. In a similar vein, there are two divergent approaches to management (Höpfl, 1994): the rhetorical, oriented towards persuasion, and the poetic, equipped with the potential to subvert and question power and its structures. Rhetorics strives to hide ambiguity and aims to direct toward a linear and fixed course. Poetics opens horizons, burst out of categories, helps to see what is under the surface. However, Heather Höpfl warned her readers that the poetic should not be seen as a resource to be used for the purposes of management. It transcends by far the narrow notions of standards and objectives. Poetics is a spontaneous cultural force that helps to embrace ambiguity and ambivalence in order to seek genuine inspiration – that is, allowing oneself to be connected to something greater than ourselves, to transcend the everyday but not becoming disrespectful towards it. A connection with a greater whole helps us to use imagination and higher emotions. Thus, true creativity becomes possible – not the tired management slogan, but the respectful receptivity that characterises real creation. At the same time, the poetic experience makes people sensitive towards the emergence of bonds and relationships and thus has the potential to unite, even in social settings which have been subjected to divisive management practices. Poetics, by cultivating ambiguity, contribute to the building of profound bonds and accord without levelling difference and uniqueness. All too often the poetic is managed out of our work organizations by the practice of an obsessive filling in of empty spaces (Höpfl, 1995b).

Poetics is not an expendable luxury, a path towards self-actualisation, but a necessity nowadays, in the era of a failing capitalist system. It brings the hope of real sustainability. Heather Höpfl (1995b) points out that rhetorics may present themselves as the effective management strategy (and of course it will), but by reducing complexity and ambiguity, they make organizations more vulnerable. Silence and attention open the mind towards poetics. In organized settings this lends voice to the margins, important for the search of future possibilities, as well as an understanding for the whole, both of which are central to an organization's ability to renew itself. Getting rid of poetics means forsaking self-regeneration and restitution in a situation of crisis.

Making room for poetics in organizations is not the same thing as just providing an empty space. Emptiness may be living or dead – a form of ordering, cleansing, eradicating all disorganization. Poetics thrives in a living emptiness, flourishing with difference and otherness:

> In poetics the meaning is always ambivalent and resonates with the flux of experience.
>
> (Höpfl, 1995b, p. 176)

Such emptiness invites poetic experience, which is always rhythmical and resilient to restatement and paraphrase. It cannot be turned or translated into standards, benchmarks or rules. However, it can be easily translated into embodied, living experience which is a tension between inner and external involvements. Höpfl (ibid.) emphasises that it is always intimately interlinked with the human condition and it is on this very fundamental level that it offers a connection for all human beings through sadness, joy, tiredness, awe and so on. It is a unity of principle rather than of slogan, aim or presentation of self. Therefore, it can be so beneficial for the development of a potential for renewal that is organic, in accordance with deeper human and cultural flows, rather than coercive or merely calculated. Such renewal may work even in situations of hopeless crises, of dead ends and exhaustion.

This is the very core of humanistic management. It relies on an approach to change that springs from human nature and that is in accordance with cultural dynamics. Language itself can be instrumental in a reorientation towards such management (Höpfl, 2000). The adoption of poetic language opens a communicational space that in itself welcomes experience and openness to regenerative currents of culture. By the rejection of the postulate of obsessive ordering, the introduction of such language helps social actors reclaim their natural need and desire for movement, change, creativity. As the Greek etymology of the word *metaphor* suggests, adopting metaphoric thinking may help to find new direction.

> It is in the relationship between movement and metaphor, with the latter as the vehicle for movement or carriage, that the possibility of exploring motivation (as movement), emotion (as movement) passion (as bearing and as phoria) and expressive behaviour (as meta-phor) becomes apparent. Metaphor is about movement.
>
> (ibid., p. 26)

Metaphor can bring back the now almost lost function of professional judgement to organizations, as it has the ability to bring back the balance between different and unequivocal elements of the organization, such as public trust, the claim of knowledge, motivation, experience and structure (Höpfl, 2000; 2005). The rhetorics of change must be replaced by the poetics of change if we are ever to create living sustainable organizations. Living emptiness, ready to hold poetic language and a poetics of change, can be invoked and embraced by the means of aesthetic interventions. Stephen Linstead and Heather Höpfl (2000) propose the aesthetic perspective as a viable alternative to the linear reductionist logic of the currently dominant management models. It offers a constructive approach to filling in the gap between world perception and human experience, which now seems to be an inevitable side effect of a rationalistic science and organization.

Making use of metaphors and poetics without deep respect and poetic consciousness, can result in further mismanagement. Heather Höpfl (1992) speaks of methods reminding of religious missionary activity, utilised by managers towards employees, promising values that will not be delivered in the capitalist business context and aimed at extracting dedication and identification. Feelings close to religious conversion are induced but what such management in reality offers is a mirage, a fraudulent replacement for salvation and meaning. Such methods can possibly be more harmful for human well-being and a sustainable business culture, as they erode trust, extort enthusiasm for the price of burnout and in the end result in what we are dealing with today: a culture of lies ("posttruth") and deception.

Reductionist methods, increasingly presented as an effective replacement of a management concerned with human relations, will not fulfil this role satisfactorily, predicted Heather Höpfl in an article (2002c) dedicated to managerial initiatives such as quality management, benchmarking and strategic approaches to human resource development. Organizations adopt such methods as response to the need, usually profoundly unconscious, to find the lost archetype of the Anima, the suppressed feminine element. The Anima is the female aspect of the soul (and Animus – the male), containing roles that women traditionally play in culture. In most societies both the Anima and the Animus are present in cultural expressions and each person's soul contains both, in the conscious or unconscious domain. However, contemporary organizations are increasingly disposing of any viable expressions of the female soul, turning it into a profoundly unconscious thrust of loss and desire. The quest becomes something of a search of the Holy Grail, only without the sincerity, deference or even consciousness of what is being at stake and for what reason. This unspoken ideal cannot become genuinely inspiring, because it remains hidden and repressed. Unless Anima is brought back in full conscious light to management and organizing, feelings of melancholy and loss will persevere and deepen as a collective and individual response to such initiatives.

In the relentless pursuit of future states, organizations as purposive entities seek to construct for themselves the empty emblems of the object of the quest. . . . Strategy gives birth to more strategy, rhetoric to more rhetoric and text to more text and so on. The sublime is never attained.

(ibid., p. 18)

Coda

And so it is time to end this short text on our colleague, our friend, professor Heather Höpfl, one of the most original and inspiring scholars we have met, a tremendous influence on people and ideas, reaching a long way beyond existing institutions and fashions. She was one of a kind, not one to be measured, indexed, classified, put into boxes. She would have liked this: a Greek man and a Polish woman, celebrating her by invoking dots and sparking pantographs, in a text written so absolutely out of tune with current formats and trends that one can wonder *what* they were thinking, it looks quite unpublishable. As we wrote it, we cried a little, we smiled a little and we took heart from doing it, which we can share with our readers. As Heather liked to say: *resistance is good for the heart, we should insist to remain human.*

Image 5.4 Heather Höpfl in Växjö, Sweden, 2007

Notes

1 She really liked dots.
2 For Heather Höpfl's biography, please see www.timeshighereducation.com/news/people/obituaries/heather-hpfl-1948-2014/2015724.article.
3 See also the special issue of *Culture and Organization* (2017) dedicated to Heather Höpfl's contribution to the field.

Recommended reading

Original text by Höpfl

Höpfl, Heather (2000), The suffering mother and the miserable son: Organising women and organising women's writing. *Gender, Work and Organisations*, 7(2): 98–105.

Key academic text

Linstead, Stephen and Heather Höpfl (2000), *The Aesthetics of Organization*. London: Sage.

Other resource

Czarniawska, Barbara and Höpfl Heather (2002), *Casting the Other: The Production and Maintenance of Inequalities in Work Organizations*. London: Routledge.

References

Boncori, I. (2017), Mission impossible: A reading of the after-death of the heroine. *Culture and Organization*, 23(2): 95–109.
Brecht, B. (1964), *Brecht on Theatre: The Development of Aesthetic*. London: Methuen Drama.
Brook, P. (1968), *The Empty Space*, New York: Atheneum
Czarniawska, B. and H. Höpfl (2002), *Casting the Other: The Production and Maintenance of Inequalities in Work Organizations*. London: Routledge.
Goffman, E. (1959), *The Presentation of Self in Everyday Life*. London: Penguin Books.
Hjorth, D. and M. Kostera (eds.) (2007), *Entrepreneurship and the Experience Economy*. Frederiksberg: Copenhagen Business School.
Höpfl, H. (1992), The making of the corporate acolyte: Some thoughts on charismatic leadership and the reality of organizational commitment. *Journal of Management Studies*, 29(1): 23–33.
Höpfl, H. (1994), Learning by heart: The rules of rhetoric and the poetics of experience. *Management Learning*, 25(3): 463–474.
Höpfl, H. (1995a), Performance and customer service: The cultivation of contempt. *Studies in Cultures, Organizations and Societies*, 1(1): 47–62.

Höpfl, H. (1995b), Organisational rhetoric and the threat of ambivalence. *Studies in Cultures, Organizations and Societies*, 1(2): 175–187.

Höpfl, H. (2000), The Aesthetics of Reticence. In Stephen Linstead and Heather Hopfl (eds) *The Aesthetics of Organization.* London: Sage, 93–110.

Höpfl, H. (2002a), Organizational Theatre and the Site of Performance. *Organizations as Theatre and Organizational Theatre: From Metaphor to Intervention*, Academy of Management Symposium, Washington.

Höpfl, H. (2002b), Playing the part: Reflections on aspects of mere performance in the customer-client relationship. *Journal of Management Studies*, 39(2): 255–267.

Höpfl, H. (2002c), Strategic quest and the search for the primal mother. *Human Resource Development International*, 5(1): 11–22.

Höpfl, H. (2000d), On being moved. *Studies in Cultures, Organizations and Societies*, 6(1): 15–34.

Höpfl, H. (2005), Indifference. In: W. C. Jones and D. O'Doherty (red.) *Manifestos: For the Business School of Tomorrow.* Åbo: Dvalin Books, 61–71.

Höpfl, H., C. Steyaert, S. Meisiek, D. Hjorth, H. Hansen and D. Bille (2006), In the wings: On the possibility of theatrical space. *Journal of Critical Postmodern Organization Science*, 5(3–4): 93–98.

Kazantzakis, N. (2000), *Zorba the Greek.* London: Faber and Faber.

Kostera, M. (2000), A letter from the empty stage. *Studies in Cultures, Organizations and Societies*, 6: 1–5.

Kostera, M. (2016), Humanistic management. In: Barbara Czarniawska (ed.) *A Research Agenda for Management and Organization Studies.* Cheltenham: Edward Elgar, 38–48.

Linstead, S. and H. Höpfl (2000), *The Aesthetics of Organization.* London: Sage.

Pine, J. and J. Gilmore (1999), *The Experience Economy: Work Is Theatre & Every Business a Stage.* Boston: Harvard Business School Press.

Schreyögg, G. and H. Höpfl (2004), Theatre and organization: Editorial introduction, *Organization Studies*, 25(5): 691–704.

6 Discursive writing, representations of the past and gender

Writing Frances Perkins out of management and organizational studies

Kristin S. Williams and Albert J. Mills

The overwhelming argument and thought which made me do it in the end in spite of personal difficulties was the realization that the door might not be opened to a woman again for a long, long time, and that I had a kind of duty to other women to walk in and sit down on the chair that was offered, and so establish the right of others long hence and far distant to sit in the high seat – Frances Perkins on her appointment as United States Secretary of Labour.

(as cited in Keller, 2006: 78)

Frances Perkins served as the United States Secretary of Labor from 1933 to 1944 under President Franklin D. Roosevelt (FDR). She was instrumental in ushering in the New Deal[1] and the measures that formed the basis of social welfare policy in the United States for decades to come. These programs focused on such things as the forty-hour workweek, minimum wage, worker's compensation, unemployment insurance, laws banning child labour, unemployment relief, social security and public works. Many contemporary accounts have sought to revise "history" and recast her as a leader in public administration, a feminist hero, a civil rights activist and a lost proto-management theorist (e.g. Burnier, 2008; Newman, 2004; Downey, 2009; and Guzda, 1980; Prieto et al., 2016; Williams and Mills, 2017, respectively[2]). In this chapter, we examine and contrast accounts of various storytellers on the subject and status of Perkins in relation to the field of management and organizations. In the process, we map and deconstruct the associated discourses that facilitate or inhibit our ability to embrace Perkins as a Management and Organization Studies (MOS) scholar.

Desperately seeking Frances

Unless you look very hard, you might not learn of Perkins's accomplishments at all. The moniker of "the first female cabinet secretary" is often the beginning and the end of a citation in history books about Perkins. For those who have delved deeper and attempted to tell her story, we will argue that they have done so discursively, assigning a subject position and constructing an identity, which has contributed to the production of a ghost figure.

Elsewhere, we have argued that Perkins's work as a proto-management theorist was overlooked and supressed by several discourses, including that of gender, and social phenomena such as the New Deal and the settlement ethos (see Williams and Mills, 2017). We found that Perkins contributions were largely credited to male scholars in the emergent field of MOS that focused largely on business concerns before broader humanitarian concerns (Burrell and Morgan, 1979; Calás and Smircich, 1996b; Foster, Mills, and Weatherbee, 2014; Williams and Mills, 2018). In this earlier investigation, we uncovered the following management theories and practices employed by Perkins:

1   A *conference style of engagement* which is a method she used to great effect to reach consensus over otherwise intractable problems and conflicts (Newman, 2004);
2   *Investigation, research and experimentation*, which Perkins used to bridge the gap between theory and practice and create informed legislation and labour agreements (Perkins, 1934);
3   An emphasis on *pride and craft* and *education*, to avoid deskilling and displacement of workers and to address the rise in technology's influence on the workplace (Perkins, 1934);
4   *Management strategies* that favoured *self-governance* and *partnerships* built on trust and mutual accountability, which had a powerful effect in negotiations with trade unions and industry (Perkins, 1934);
5   *Economic principles*, which incorporated social work philosophies such as the *theory of abundance* (Patten, 1907) which greatly favoured the idea of a surplus economy with increased per capita production, shorter working hours, higher wages and a better quality of life (Perkins, 1934); and
6   *Stabilisation* through *relief measures* and *sustainability planning*, whereby she promoted government and industry to work together to create a balance between consumption and production through "socially desirable practices" (Perkins, 1934: 140).

In this chapter, we explore how Perkins became "lost" to the study of management and organization. This investigation is meant to help us understand the processes which made Perkins invisible in the first place.

By unravelling, contesting and deconstructing some of the most commonly cited moments in the life of the first female cabinet secretary in the United States, we will show how her socially constructed identity further subverted the opportunity for her to be a more broadly known and powerful historical figure. In this chapter, we are asking the question: does the way Frances Perkins has been socially constructed (written about, or not written about) help explain why she has been largely overlooked? We also believe that the ways in which Perkins has been social constructed reveal the discursive ways we continue to construct female leaders today, thus limiting new understandings.

Theory and methodology

As feminist and aspiring feminist poststructuralists,[3] we are concerned with presenting the perspectives of women, though we cannot escape our own subjectivity as researchers and enthusiasts of Perkins. Our position is epistemologically salient (Scharff, 2010; Alcoff, 1995). We also believe that power relations structure all areas of life (Weedon, 1997). These structures may pre-exist us and determine subject positions, or ways of being an individual with associated values and expected behaviour (Weedon, 1997). We are concerned with theories of language, subjectivity and power and challenging what constitutes useful knowledge while simultaneously accessing and questioning knowledge that is already constituted (Weedon, 1997). Through this theoretical lens, we can gain insight into how meaning has been produced and reproduced – specifically, how dominant discourses that reinforce subject positions can expose the marginalisation that has resulted.

Poststructuralism assumes that meaning is constituted in language, and meaning is acquired but always attached to historically specific discourses (Weedon, 1997). These discourses (e.g. gender) fix subjects and meaning in contexts, which are sometimes limiting or even competing. The attempt in this form of theory is not to find a specific truth, but rather disrupt, contest and critique; favouring the production of new, specific knowledges with specific implications (Weedon, 1997).

Employed here as a set of methodologies which explore how discursive structures "play a crucial role in the expression, construction, confirmation and hence the reproduction of social inequality" (Van Dijk, 2008: 5), critical discourse analysis (CDA) will take this investigation deeper with an emphasis on context and critique. We will follow the lead of other CDA researchers, who have used a Foucauldian-informed stance, which focuses on "unmasking the privileges inherent in particular discourses" (Phillips and Hardy 2002: 21).

Our discursive focus

There are many key moments in Perkins's life that have been drawn on to give insight into her leadership. We exam selected examples of those moments to reveal their discursive character and to help explain why Perkins is not a more conspicuous figure in MOS. Our major concern here is not so much to fit Perkins into a pre-given field (Calás and Smircich, 1996a) but rather to explore how that field developed through a largely masculinist, ahistorical and managerialist lens (Burrell and Morgan, 1979; Calás and Smircich, 1996b) and what are the implications for feminist organizational analysis.

The list

A fixture in any portrait of Perkins is reference to *a list* she presented to FDR upon his request to have her join his cabinet. The list refers to Perkins's agenda, which included a forty-hour workweek, minimum wage, ending child labour, worker's compensation, social security, public works and more! Kaye and Gibbon (2011) paint the exchange as a kind of ultimatum, whereby Perkins told FDR she would only take the post if he backed her on the goals she had recorded on a piece of paper. Cohen as cited in Perkins (1946: xii) softens the framing slightly by suggesting that "Perkins brought along a list of the causes she had been fighting for and told Roosevelt she would take the job only if he agreed to back all of them". Severn (1976: 110) relays the exchange as follows:

> Frances told him that, if she accepted the position of secretary of labour, there was a great deal more that she wanted to accomplish. She then produced a list of proposals for labour legislation and economic improvement. Before she gave him her answer, she wanted to be sure she would have his support, and she wondered whether he might not consider the program too ambitious to undertake.

Newman (2004) presents this as a professional exchange in which Perkins laid out her reform agenda to the president as a condition of her appointment. Newman (2004: 92) then adds a comment of her own: "if this represented the feminization of the department, so be it". This remark is not attributed to Perkins. This overlay of subjectivity speaks more to Newman's objectives in framing Perkins than to Perkins or FDR. The differences in accounts are fascinating, painting Perkins on the one hand as shrewd and forceful and on the other hand as professional, but with a clandestine feminist agenda. Such differences in accounts create the potential for further multiplicity in their retelling; retelling, which can serve to enhance or play down Perkins's potential contribution to the emergent field of management and organizational studies. There appears to be more focus on how this agenda was presented and negotiated and not what was in it! We respect and appreciate the desire and attempt to cast Perkins as a hero of social reform, however, in so doing, attention is taken away from the agenda itself and ultimately the success Perkins had in achieving each of these goals.

To add additional context, this was not the first time Perkins had discussed an agenda before accepting a post with FDR. When Roosevelt was named governor of New York and enlisted Perkins as Industrial Commissioner in 1929, she also had specific things she wanted to accomplish, which she presented to FDR in advance. Perkins gives us an indication of the reception by quoting FDR: "I want all these things done. Make all your plans – go as far as you can. When you need help, come to me and I will do everything I can. I am for the program – all of it" (Perkins 1946: 58; Pasachoff 1999: 58; Colman 1993: 50). It frankly seems unbelievable that a pair that worked so well together and had known each other since 1910 would find themselves toe-to-toe over "a list" in 1933.

In a less theatrical recitation, Martin (1976) reveals that Perkins was reticent about accepting the appointment but had over several months compiled a handful of notes. In her meeting with FDR, she at first tried to decline his offer, but when he refused she said "I should want to do a great deal" (Colman 1993: 60). She continued: "I have written out a few notes . . . I won't hold you to this. But I don't want to say yes to you unless you know what I'd like to do and are willing to have me go ahead and try" (Perkins, cited in Martin 1976: 239–240). This is hardly an ultimatum and those that have reconstructed the exchange as something else have had an agenda in mind. To what end? Is what she did accomplish and the way she did it not enough? The list would in fact be the mandate of the Department of Labor for the next five years with virtually all agenda points accomplished by 1938.

Immigration portfolio

One of Perkins's first steps as Secretary of Labor was to clean up the Immigration Portfolio, which was housed in Labor. This included abolishing Section 24, which under the previous secretary was viewed to be working outside the regular body of inspectors (Martin, 1976). Section 24 was run by Murray and Henry Garsson and was actively concerned with finding and deporting illegal immigrants, especially alleged Communists (Cohen, 2009). Under Perkins's leadership, she sought to simplify laws and treat immigrants "in a manner worthy of the dignity and professed humanity of the United States" (Martin, 1976: 293).

Mohr (1979: 259) suggests that the Immigration Portfolio, and specifically the file on West Coast longshoremen union leader Harry Bridges, was fodder for the press "who wrote with uncontained relish about Frances Perkins' continued demise". Burnier (2008: 408) offers this claim:

> The Bridges affair damaged Perkins as an administrator, but Roosevelt refused to accept her resignation in 1940 or 1944. Instead, he marginalized her through a series of politically motivated decisions.

The Immigration Service as well as the FBI and San Francisco Police had made an investigation of Harry Bridges, concerning allegations that he was a Communist. The case dragged on for years and preliminaries of an impeachment[4] were brought against Perkins for failing to deport Bridges. Perkins thought "Roosevelt made light of these proceedings [suggesting] 'it's all nonsense'. . . I didn't like the idea of being impeached and was considerably disturbed by the episode" (Perkins, 1946: 305). Wandersee (1993) proposes that the entire event was a political attack. The committee ultimately determined that there were no grounds to support an impeachment. Some have tried to suggest that FDR lost faith in Perkins after the failed impeachment proceedings and during the war years.[5] Martin (1976) supports these assertions by saying that despite being cleared, she was never fully able to feel vindicated because of insufficient media interest in the findings of the committee.

Of further interest, some make the connection of the impeachment charges with the move of Immigration out of Labor. Colman (1993) offers that FDR did not consult Perkins about the move of Immigration from Labor to Justice, but acknowledges that Perkins had been suggesting it should be moved for the last five years. Perkins is quite clear on what occurred at the time: "the president didn't walk over me on that. That was following out my recommendation, somewhat belatedly" (Perkins as cited in Pasachoff, 1999: 111). In her biography of FDR she references the transfer of Immigration in the following way:

> I had been recommending for five years that the Immigration Service be taken out of the Department of Labor and put in some more appropriate place. During the war the opportunity came to do this.
>
> (Perkins, 1946: 346)

Clearly contested interpretations existed at the time and have persisted since. Burnier's (2008) other assertion that Perkins's role was marginalised is also disputed by Perkins herself:

> The Department of Labor was not weakened during the war. It was strengthened. It got larger appropriations. Special technical duties of all sorts were assigned to it by the Congress and the President.
>
> (Perkins, 1946: 346)

These events further denied Perkins an advantage with public opinion or the press. Did these events contribute to her marginalisation? Oddly, in the case of US Presidents Clinton, Johnson and Nixon, the impeachment process appears to have elevated, not diminished, their status in history (whether good or bad).

Perkins on FDR

Perkins's relationship with FDR was complex but central to the success they both had in the New Deal program. She was not immediately impressed with him when they first met, especially because he did not support the 54-Hour Bill in 1912 – one of the first legislative attempts to address work-week standards. Some have taken liberty to paint these initial impressions hastily and critically. Cohen as cited in Perkins (1946: ix) suggests that "Roosevelt had struck her as something of a spoiled aristocrat who lacked compassion for those who were less well off".

When FDR contracted polio, he lost the use of his legs. He fought back to moderate health and resumed political life. His illness appears to have changed him in her eyes. In her words, she describes FDR as having underwent a "spiritual transformation during the years of illness . . . [having] purged the slightly arrogant attitude he had displayed on occasion before he was stricken" (Perkins, 1946: 29). She adds, "and it was in those accommodations to necessity that Franklin Roosevelt began to approach the stature of humility and inner integrity which made him truly great" (Perkins, 1946: 45). Cohen's views do not align with Perkins's own account and Cohen may, arguably, have intentionally exaggerated for dramatic effect.

Perkins was critical of FDR. It would seem she was quite direct with him about his shortcomings, but in an intelligent and didactic way. When as governor of the State of New York, he invited her to become the state's Industrial Commissioner, she recalls that FDR was quite pleased with himself and boasted that he was even more liberal than former Governor Al Smith (who had originally appointed her to be a member of the Industrial Commission). Per Martin (1976: 205), Perkins cites FDR as saying, "Al would never have thought of making a woman the head of the department", to which she responded:

> But it was more of a victory of Al to bring himself to appoint a woman, never appointed before, when I was unknown, than it is for you when I have a record as a responsible public officer for almost ten years.
>
> (Perkins, cited in Pasachoff, 1999: 57)

Despite this exchange liberally quoted by many authors, there still seems to be the contention that she was not critical of him. For example, Burnier

(2008: 415) offers us the following insight when referring to Perkins biography of FDR: "indeed she was willing to be a 'docile body' for Roosevelt in that she is never critical of him". In her 1946 biography, *The Roosevelt I Knew*, she openly criticises FDR. Her loyalty seems to be, by others, confused with her opinion. She stipulates at the start of her biography of FDR that her book is biased and in his favour because she "agreed with most of his positions and policies and worked for many years to help develop, spread and establish them in action" (Perkins, 1946: 4). She goes on to paint a complex picture of Roosevelt:

> He was many things – not clear, not simple, with drives and compulsions in a dozen different directions, with curiosity sending him from one field and experience to another, with imagination making it possible for him to identify himself, at least partly and temporarily, with wildly different phenomena and people.
>
> (Perkins, 1946: 4)

In terms of his handling of the press, she thought that upon his appointment he had introduced them into governmental affairs too early and it was "a great mistake" (Perkins, 1946: 287). She was also cautious of his word choices when making speeches. She was concerned that he often said not quite what he meant, especially when he chose rather poorly worded phrases like "economic royalists" and suggested insensitively that people ought not to be "too rich". She disliked his demagoguery and some of his totalitarian techniques according to Martin (1976).

Perhaps where it mattered most to Perkins, on issues of labour, she was weary of his involvement on labour disputes, and offers this candid backhanded compliment:

> He was not a good negotiator in a labor dispute. He was too imaginative. He had too many ideas, and they sometimes were not in harmony with ancient policies, prejudices, and habits of the union or industry he was dealing with.
>
> (Perkins, 1946: 290)

In terms of trade unions, she offers this criticism:

> There were many things about trade unions that Roosevelt never fully understood. I doubt that he understood what solidarity really means in the trade union movement.
>
> (Perkins, 1946: 311)

In terms of his understanding of labour issues, she is quick to suggest how limited his grasp of the complexity of matters were:

> The President rarely knew more about the situation when he made a proposal to the two sides in this formal way than what could be put down on half a sheet of paper by the Secretary of Labor or others having jurisdiction.
>
> (Perkins, 1946: 313)

The superficial view that Perkins was not critical of FDR and passive in her manner is highly suspicious and likely contributes to diminishing her prominence in the New Deal mandate relative to FDR. Our impression of these varied insights and countless others we could share, is one of a complex, honest, humour-filled and enduring partnership that is difficult to summarise. What we do learn by examining how Perkins speaks of FDR is that she consistently positioned herself in the shadow of FDR and indeed she seemed quite content for him to enjoy the limelight, seldom seeking credit for the work accomplished under his presidency. Thus, history records many of their successes as his.

FDR on Perkins

Given the varied opinions about Perkins in general, it is important before exploring those views further that we offer some insight into FDR's views of Perkins. Some have suggested he was cold to her and left her alone in her battles. Downey (2009) suggests that he took no action to publicly support her during the impeachment proceeding. But it is our view that Perkins seems to feel she had considerable latitude and trust from FDR: "he had come to have confidence in me. It was a very personal relationship. That was all there was to it" (Perkins, cited in Pasachoff, N (1999): 118). Given that Perkins was one of the longest-serving cabinet secretaries in history (next to Harold Ickes and James Wilson) and one of only two to stay the duration of FDR's presidency (next to Harold Ickes), we believe that also speaks broadly about FDR's views and respect of Perkins. When she boldly questioned President Hoover's unemployment statistics in 1930 by issuing a statement in rebuttal to one that appeared on the front page of the *New York Times*, she became concerned that she had acted in haste, only to find a cheerful Roosevelt who exclaimed: "Bully for you! That was a fine statement and I am glad you made it" (Roosevelt, cited in Perkins, 1946: 93).

When Perkins attempted to resign in 1936, FDR refused to accept it, joking: "Well, I don't think it would be so good politically. I notice that we haven't lost the labor vote or the women's vote on your account" (cited in Perkins, 1946: 131). In 1940, when she attempted to resign again, FDR said to her: "you keep me guarded against a lot of things that no new man walking in here would protect me from" (cited in Colman, 1993: 95). In 1944, she was desperate for a change, but he insisted she stay on, offering this plea: "Frances, you can't go now. You mustn't put this on me now. I just can't be bothered now. I can't think of anybody else, and I can't get used to anybody else. Not now!" (Perkins, 1946: 377). Modestly, she offers the opinion of herself that "however much of a pain I might be to some people, the majority of voters had not reacted unfavourably to my programs" (Perkins, 1946: 131).

It was her opinion that FDR sought on a variety of critical issues (e.g. regarding appointment of various officials such as the administrator to public works). During wartime, he relied on her to sort out administrative tangles and remove conflict between agencies. That became her focus in these years. FDR said "you take the lead . . . in getting them together" (Perkins, 1946: 346). Then he would direct heads of agencies to "go straighten it out. See the Secretary of Labor" (Perkins, 1946: 365).

FDR also appreciated when Perkins thought ahead to secure measures of the New Deal, should and when the National Industrial Recovery Act died. She said to the president during one of the conferences about the fate of the Act, "never mind . . . I've got two bills which will do everything you and I think are important under NRA. . . . I have them locked up in the lower left-hand drawer of my desk against an emergency" (Perkins, 1946: 238).

In one of their final conversations, he offered what she has stated are the most beautiful words he said to her. She recalls in her biography of him:

> "Frances, you have done awfully well. I know what you have been through. I know what you have accomplished. Thank you". He put his hand over mine and gripped it. There were tears in our eyes. It was all the reward that I could ever have asked – to know that he had recognized the storms and trials I had faced in developing our program, to know that he appreciated the program and thought well of it, and that he was grateful.
>
> (Perkins, 1946: 377)

Despite the praise that FDR seems to bestow on Perkins, we are only aware of these insights through her chronicles of him. Had FDR made a more public attempt to defend and praise her work, we suspect she might be more well-known.

The widely contested views of Perkins

The opinions of Perkins are vast and varied and have changed significantly over time. One of our observations is that writers have attempted to reconstruct a history in which Perkins can deservingly live on as a highly respected civil leader. At the time of her life, both early days in social work and legislative advocacy and later in government, her decisions and actions were highly criticised.

From 1936, an article and sketch appearing in an issue of *The Nation* by Paul W. Ward reads in part: "Fannie is not a policy-maker and never has been one. She lacks the imagination. More especially, she lacks the courage" (Keller, 2006: 108). Some have suggested that she struggled with public relations skills, which worked against her identity development in the press (Keller, 2006; Martin, 1976; Colman, 1993). Colman (1993: 62) says she bristled in response to personal questions from reporters by saying, "Is that quite necessary? . . . We New Englanders keep ourselves to ourselves".

Featured on the cover of *Time* magazine in 1933, her work was applauded and her appointment was credited to her work during the steel strikes (Colman, 1993). Jane Addams of Hull House wrote that "perhaps no one in the United States is better equipped for the duties of secretary of labor . . . her appointment would confer distinction and honor upon women throughout the nation" (cited in Severn, 1976: 107). Her friend and colleague, US Senator Robert Wagner, said: "Frances Perkins was, and still is, the supreme student of social conditions and remedial social legislation. She uncovered the facts and told us what to do about them" (cited in Colman, 1993: 105).

But where there was a single compliment, there appeared a more powerful critique. Martin (1976: 324) shares that many of the critiques took the line that "a two-fisted man would stand up more to labor, or that she coddled aliens because of her soft woman's heart". William Green, president of the powerful American Federation of Labor (AFL), offered this opinion of her appointment: "labor can never become reconciled to the selection" (cited in Keller, 2006: 780). The following appeared in the *Baltimore Sun* and *Washington Evening Star*:

> Call it a day boys; call it a day. The lady is better than you are and we should not be a bit surprised if higher compliments could be paid her. What's more, she is not afraid of you. And that makes an awful combination. A woman smarter than a man is something to get on guard about. But a woman smarter than a man and also not afraid of a man, well, good night!
>
> (Martin, 1976: 301)

Limitations were acknowledged by women labour activists, such as Mary Anderson, who said of Perkins:

> So every time there was a chance to single out women, she leaned over backward not to do it. I understood her difficulties and sympathized with her, but just the same it was discouraging not to have more enthusiastic backing.
>
> (cited in Mohr, 1979: 200)

The critiques were often contradictory, suggesting she was either too soft or too hard. And often the compliments were tempered, such as this one from fellow Secretary Garner, who while speaking of Perkins's performance in the first cabinet meeting said:

> I guess she's all right . . . she didn't interrupt. She didn't butt in. She didn't ask any questions. She kept still until the President asked her what she had to say. Then she said it. She said it loud enough so I could hear. She said it plain and distinct. She said it short. When she was through, she stopped. I guess she's all right.
>
> (Martin, 1976: 34)

It was not until the end of her career and beyond that there has been a sincere effort to give Perkins a fairer evaluation, which is arguably the fate of many leading female figures over time. Some of these have been almost too enthusiastic and thick with agenda. But even these need to be contextualised in the time they were made, such as this one from President John F. Kennedy at the time of his service:

> The program which Madam Perkins put forward when she became Secretary of Labor – things which we now take for granted in both political parties which were regarded as dangerous and revolutionary and things which must be fought for in the short space of 30 years ago. They were controversial and Madam Perkins, who looked so quiet and peaceful and sweet was also one of the most controversial, dangerous figures that roamed the United States in the 1930s.
>
> (cited in Mohr, 1979: 294)

Some retracted early opinions, such as John L. Lewis, president of the United Mine Workers of America (UMWA), who had called Perkins "woozy in the head", suggesting later in the *United Mine Workers Journal* that "despite all the criticism that has been hurled against her, she has performed her work within the confines of the limitations imposed upon her mighty well" (cited in Mohr, 1979: 278). This supports our assertion that meaning is indeed not fixed and the social construction of identity and history is an ongoing process.

Upon news of Perkins's death, many opinions had softened and there were several fitting tributes, including this one from then Secretary of Labor W. Willard Wirtz:

> Every man and woman in America who works at a living wage, under safe conditions, for reasonable hours or who is protected by unemployment insurance or social security is Frances Perkins' debtor.
>
> (cited in Lawson, 1966: 153)

Of her time in office, she simply offers "I came to work for God, FDR and the millions of forgotten, plain, common working men [and women]" (Perkins, cited in Downey, 2009: 398). We assert that her modesty coupled with her gender, and the voices of proxies and critics, have contributed to her invisibility in history. Even on her epitaph (and at her request), a final record of her voice on her tombstone simply (and insufficiently) reads:

Frances Perkins Wilson
1880–1965
Secretary of Labor of USA
1933–1944

Conclusion

In this chapter, we have sought to untangle and contest some assertions made of Frances Perkins. Our efforts here have not been to assert a single truth, but reveal that what exists are several competing, contested and contrived histories (Jenkins, 1991; Munslow, 2010). Thus, we have been concerned with highlighting that there are motives that persist in the social construction of an identity; motives that are located in material practices and social contexts that are read and experienced discursively. This process of social construction is ongoing, and we as authors are now also a part of that process where Perkins is concerned. Our aim, however, was to reveal the seemingly innocuous ways that writers can subjugate power through language; how authors can construct identity and reproduce it for broader consumption; how writers can reinforce a subject position; and finally, how writers can deny the voice of the subject by overlaying their own subjectivity.

Perkins has been denied prominence in history, which has meant that we have not benefited from the lessons that come from her experiences in the early days of social work, in government, as a legislator and as a pioneer female leader. But the relationship of history to the past, we contend, is highly problematic (Durepos and Mills, 2012; Williams and Mills, 2018). These circumstances of social construction are amenable to change. In the case of Perkins, it was not only the way she was written about but also the way she was not written about that contributed to her becoming a ghost figure. Those who wield the power to construct histories and create new knowledge need to be mindful of what they include, what they disregard and for whom they write. Our message in this chapter is to be steadfast in our critique of history and look closely at those that are celebrated, and look even closer at those that have been overlooked. When women take up malestream roles, there persists a drive to subjugate them back into subject positions which are consistent with taken-for-granted gender attributes and behaviour. These discursive profiles result in more attention paid to what someone should be doing versus what they are actually doing, causing lost opportunities to study, learn and appreciate the contributions of female leaders, past and present.

We conclude with a plea for more attention to and analysis of the role of history in the gendering of management and organizational studies. This entails an examination not simply of the gendered processes involved in the social construction of leadership but of the problem of history itself. Following Jenkins (1991), we view history as discursive, that is, that accounts of the past are ontologically unobtainable except through their association with history, which serves to legitimize them – what Munslow (2010) refers to as the past as history. Thus, to examine the gendered nature of accounts of the past, we arguably need also to simultaneously examine the gendered nature of history itself (Hartt, Durepos, Mills, and Helms Mills, 2017). To do otherwise would be to recover the leadership qualities of Perkins and other female leaders only to incorporate them in masculinist frameworks of history, much as was the case of Mary Parker Follett (Calás and Smircich, 1996b).

Notes

1 A series of socio-economic programs introduced by the Roosevelt administration, largely between 1933 and 1938. The New Deal was the campaign promise of Franklin D. Roosevelt to address the economic and social issues of the Great Depression. See, for example, Hiltzik (2011).
2 In addition to various published sources, we also searched through housed collections or archives, including the Franklin D. Roosevelt Presidential Library and Museum, the Frances Perkins Centre and the Columbia University Oral History Museum.
3 To be clear, our male second author is tentatively and "aspirationally" applying this designation to recognise (1) the dangers of incorporation and silencing

involved in the socio-politics of labelling, (2) the unattainable but constant value in attempting to identity/associate with feminism, and (3) the understanding that feminism is never a fixed point but is itself subject to radical changes over time (Mills, 2006).

4 In 1939, many of Perkins's actions on behalf of Labor angered conservatives and the House Un-American Activities Committee brought an impeachment resolution against her after she refused to deport Harry Bridges. The impeachment proceedings were eventually dropped for lack of evidence (e.g. see American Federation of Labor and Congress of Industrial Organizations, AFL-CIO).

5 This is an area of future research, as a recent study suggests that the war years exacerbated perceived needs for more masculine displays of leadership (Costigliola, 2012).

Recommended reading

Original text by Perkins

Perkins, F. (1934) *People at work*. New York, NY: John Day.

Key academic text

Williams, K. S. and Mills A. J. (2017) Frances Perkins: gender, context and history in the neglect of a management theorist. *Journal of Management History*, *23*(1), 32–50.

Accessible resources

Martin, G (1976) *Madam secretary Frances Perkins*. Boston: Houghton Mifflin.
Perkins, F. Reminiscences of Frances Perkins in the Oral History Research Office Collection of the Columbia University Libraries (OHRO/CUL).

References

Alcoff, L. (1995) The problem of speaking for others. In Roof, J. and Wiegman, R. (Eds.), *Who can speak? Authority and critical identity*. Urbana: University of Illinois Press, pp. 97–111.

Burnier, D. (2008) Frances Perkins' disappearance from American public administration: A genealogy of marginalization. *Administrative Theory & Praxis*, *30*(4), 398–423.

Burrell, G. and Morgan, G. (1979) *Sociological paradigms and organizational analysis*. London: Heinemann.

Calás, M. B. and Smircich, L. (1996a) From 'The Woman's' point of view: Feminist approaches to organization studies. In Clegg, S. R., Hardy, C. and Nord, W. R. (Eds.), *Handbook of organization studies*. London: Sage, pp. 218–257.

Calás, M. B. and Smircich, L. (1996b) Not ahead of her time: Reflections on Mary Parker Follett as prophet of management. *Organization*, *3*(1): 147–152.

Cohen, A. (2009) *Nothing to fear: FDR's inner circle and the hundred days that created modern America.* New York: Penguin Press.

Colman, P. (1993) *A woman unafraid: The achievements of Frances Perkins.* New York: ASJA Press.

Downey, K. (2009) *The woman behind the New Deal: The life of Frances Perkins, FDR's Secretary of Labor and his moral conscience.* New York: Anchor.

Durepos, G. and Mills, A. J. (2012) *Anti-history: Theorizing the past, history, and historiography in management and organization studies.* Charlotte, NC: Information Age.

Foster, J., Mills, A. J. and Weatherbee, T. G. (2014) History, field definition and management studies: The case of the New Deal. *Journal of Management History,* 20(2), 179–199.

Guzda, H. P. (1980) Frances Perkins' interest in a New Deal for blacks. *Monthly Labor Review,* 103: 31–35.

Hartt, C. M., Durepos, G., Mills, A. J. and Helms Mills, J. (2017) Performing the past: Anti-history, gendered spaces and feminist practice. In: Mills, A. J. *Insights and Research on the study of gender and intersectionality in international airline culture.* Bradford: Emerald Books.

Hiltzik, M. (2011) *The new deal: A modern history.* New York: Free Press.

Jenkins, K. (1991) *Re-thinking history.* London: Routledge.

Kaye, J. and Gibbon, P. (2011) *Teaching American history: The woman behind the new deal by Kirstin Downey* [lecture], Available from: http://heroesinamerica.org/ssecamoreperfectunion/PDFs/kaye_frances_perkins.pdf

Keller, E. (2006) *Frances Perkins: First woman cabinet member.* Greensboro, NC: Morgan Reynolds.

Lawson, D. (1966) *Frances Perkins, first lady of the cabinet.* London: Abelard-Schuman.

Martin, G. (1976) *Madam secretary Frances Perkins.* Boston: Houghton Mifflin.

Mills, A. J. (2006) *Sex, strategy and the stratosphere: Airlines and the gendering of organizational culture.* London: Palgrave Macmillan.

Mohr, L. H. (1979) *Frances Perkins, that woman in FDR's cabinet!* Darien: North River Press.

Munslow, A. (2010) *The future of history.* London: Palgrave Macmillan.

Newman, M. A. (2004) Madam Secretary Frances Perkins. In Felbinger, C. L. and Haynes, W. A. (Eds.), *Outstanding women in public administration.* Armonk, NY: M. E. Sharpe.

Pasachoff, N. (1999) *Frances Perkins: Champion of the new deal.* New York: Oxford University Press.

Patten, S. (1907) *The new basis of civilization.* London: Macmillan.

Perkins, F. (1934) *People at work.* New York, NY: John Day.

Perkins, F. (1946) *The Roosevelt I knew.* London: Penguin Books.

Phillips, N. and Hardy, C. (2002) *Discourse analysis: Investigating processes of social construction.* Thousand Oaks: Sage.

Prieto, L. C., Phipps, S.T.A., Thompson, L. R. and Smith, X. A. (2016) Schneiderman, Perkins, and the early labor movement. *Journal of Management History,* 22(1), 50–72.

Reynolds, D. (2012). Costigliola, F. (2012). Roosevelt's Lost Alliances: How Personal Politics Helped Start the Cold War. *Diplomacy & Statecraft, 23*(4), 780–782.

Scharff, C. (2010) Silencing differences. In Ryan-Flood, R. and Gill, R. (Eds.) *Secrecy and silence in the research process: Feminist reflections.* London: Routledge.

Severn, B. (1976) *Frances Perkins: A member of the cabinet.* New York: Hawthorn Books.

Van Dijk, T. A. (2008) *Discourse & power.* New York: Palgrave Macmillan.

Wandersee, W. D. (1993) I'd rather pass a law than organize a union: Frances Perkins and the reformist approach to organized labor. *Labor History,* 35: 5–32.

Weedon, C. (1997) *Feminist practice & poststructuralist theory* (2nd ed.). Malden: Blackwell.

Williams, K. S. and Mills, A. J. (2017) Frances Perkins: Gender, context and history in the neglectof a management theorist. *Journal of Management History, 23*(1), 32–50.

Williams, K. S. and Mills, A. J. (2018) Hallie Flanagan and the Federal Theater Project: A critical undoing of management history. *Journal of Management History, 24*(3), 282–299.

Index

Note: Page numbers in italics indicate figures on the corresponding pages.